Reel
to
Real

Reel to Real

The mind, through the lens of Malayalam cinema

VIDYA CHATHOTH

Notion Press

Old No. 38, New No. 6
McNichols Road, Chetpet
Chennai - 600 031

First Published by Notion Press 2016
Copyright © Vidya Chathoth 2016
All Rights Reserved.

ISBN 978-1-946129-51-2

To my father
who seeded in me the fascination for the human mind

Contents

PREFACE

Books and cinema have been my companions from as far back as I can remember. They were introduced into my world very early in life and they transformed into an integral part of my life. I could feel the experience of a book or film as vividly as real world experiences. Films, on account of the visual imagery, influenced me more than did books. I connected to these films at an unconscious level. In my mind, I would transform into the central character of these films and live the experience of the character. The experience of the film would eventually transform into my own experience.

I was unaware of the impact these films had on my mind, save for the joy of perception that they left behind. It was only in the setting of the complexities of life that I slowly deciphered the psychological value of these films. As life exposed me to challenges of a diverse nature, I found myself turning to these films for a perspective. Cinema played a significant role in helping me surpass my vulnerability and confront the challenges in life, enabling me to live out my dreams.

Randy Pausch writes in his book, *'The Last Lecture'*:

'All of the things I loved were rooted in the dreams and goals I had as a child. My uniqueness came in the specifics of all those dreams. And I had lived out my dreams, in great measure, because of things I was taught by all sorts of extraordinary people along the way.'

Cinema provided a reference for me. It helped me connect to myself- to the perceptions that characterized the dreams I weaved as a child. In a world where thought was progressively replacing emotion, it preserved my ability to feel. It transformed into such a significant influence in my life that I found myself wanting to capture its essence in the words that I wrote. I found myself indebted to the film makers who had created films that were nothing short of Psychology Textbooks. *Lohithadas, Padmarajan, Bharathan, M.T.Vasudevan Nair* and all the artists that went into the making of these films, transformed into my mentors- mentors I had never met in real life. Cinema provided me with greater insights into the human mind than did the medical literature that I imbibed. I found myself at the juncture of art and science, aware that the human mind could never be studied in isolation from its environment. It is from this interface of art and science, of mind and brain, that I write this book.

This book was primarily the outcome of the deep gratitude I felt towards these film makers. It was also triggered by the profound sense of loss I felt when I assessed the psychological value of the 'new generation films' that have dominated the Malayalam screen. I felt it was my moral responsibility to deliver the psychological essence of these films to a larger audience and to sensitize the common man to the ingredients that define good cinema. Decades have passed since the release of the films compiled in this book, but these films remain vivid and fresh in the minds of the cinema lovers of Kerala. True art must survive the test of time. It is the moral responsibility of film makers to revive good cinema and preserve the ultimate purpose of art in human life.

I hope that this book will serve as a guide to film makers and mental health professionals. I also hope it will be received with enthusiasm by those viewers who like me, are ardent fans of these films. My ultimate objective of writing this book is to fuel a movement directed at the revival of cinema that will cater to the psychological and spiritual needs of a community.

This book is divided into two sections. *Part-I* offers a psychological perspective on the films. The films are discussed in relation to the theories of personality. *Part-II* is a narrative of selected films. It takes the reader on a journey across the minds of the characters through the plot of the film.

ACKNOWLEDGEMENTS

My mother, whose contribution to my life and to the fulfilment of this dream, is immeasurable.

My brother, for accepting me as I am and for the constant encouragement in all my spiritual quests.

Madhu Eravankara and K. Jayakumar, for sparking my interest in this endeavour.

Biju Ebenezer, for providing me the opportunity to write on his project 'Malayalam Cinema and Mental illness' at his blog- https://oldmalayalamcinema.wordpress.com

Dr Shafeeq for his inputs on 'Manichithrathazhu.'

Madan, for dreaming with me.

Ramadas Menon, Malathi Menon, Sampath Madhyastha and Jai, for believing in me.

Indu Krishnan, Sruthi Prasad, Anil Chaithra, Sindu Mathew and Pranaya Bagade, for being there for me during my most trying moments.

Swathi, Sangeetha, Anusree and Akshitha, for your unconditional love.

Dr Venugopal, for being a father figure in my life.

Vinod Varghese, for being a good friend and well-wisher.

Prapti Mehta, for seeding in me the love for language and literature.

My students who have always kept my spirits high and never ceased to believe in me.

Mini Menon, Triptarth, Sunith, Uday, Taheseen, Amudhan and all my readers and fellow bloggers to whom I owe my evolution as a writer.

Anand and Ravi, who taught me to see the abundance in life, and who live on in my mind.

Geet, Sumedha, Lal, Deepa, Saritha, Sithara, Anuradha, Sumathi, Ashwija, Lalu, Vinod, Vineesh, Poornima, Soumya, Dayanand, Shilpa, Maninder, Anish, Naren, Keerthana and all my friends for their love and support.

PART I

A PSYCHOLOGICAL STUDY OF THE FILMS

Literature And Cinema: The Answer To Our Mental Health

In books, I have travelled not only to other worlds, but also into my own…

We live in an era of schedules and deadlines. All our days are full. They are packed with thoughts, activities and interactions. And yet, it is to an emptiness that we return. An emptiness that creeps stealthily into our personal and professional spaces, rising like a slow tempest, while we are busy devising the scheme of our lives. An emptiness that we attempt to drown in the illusion we create with our material accomplishments. But the emptiness remains, stealthily gnawing at our minds, erasing all residues of who we are and where we were meant to go. But we have no time to heed to this emptiness. We learn to live with it.

In the modern world, we find ourselves persistently rushed and multitasking. We are always in forward gear. In a world that delivers change at an alarming pace, we are constantly driven by the need to keep pace. Thinking has become our natural reaction to all the events in our day-to-day lives. We are always alert, attentive and poised for change. We are never still.

We no longer wait to feel. We no longer sustain our emotions long enough for them to brew into a mood that is crucial in our emotional development. We fail to realize that it is the emotional spaces of our lives that we are losing to the pace of technology. As science/technology replaces art, thought replaces emotions. We no longer feel alive for nothing permeates us enough to move us.

Where emotions once came naturally to us, we now have to be taught what to feel and how to feel. The title of an old film comes to mind: '***Aalkkoottathil Thaniye***' (*Lonely in the crowd*). That is the predicament of the modern world. We are all connected globally and round the clock, and yet we are palpably lonely in our mansions.

Today, our emotions are sharply defined, have a clear objective, and are expressed in very specific and concrete terms. What we lose in the process, is our emotional spectrum. In the modern world, all our interactions must have a reason and a goal. We rarely interact with people to savour the companionship for we cannot afford such nothingness. The idle moments that once characterized our lives- the aimless strolls, the idle conversations, the idle moments of daydreaming and fantasizing- they are obsolete in the modern world. Even hobbies must now have a goal and timeframe.

But we forget that it was in those idle spaces that emotions resided. Sublime, yet very much there.

How did we end up creating a world where we erased all our moments of warmth and togetherness? Where we no longer had the time to sit down to a meal and savour family moments? Where our children were denied a normal childhood? Where we had lost the ability to admire sunsets and starry skies?

Numbness is the epidemic of the modern world.

We are no longer sensitive to the simple joys of life for we never give them the time that is needed to brew them into happiness in our minds. It takes us a lot to feel happy or sad. Also, happiness in this era translates to excitement or exhilaration. We are no longer sensitive to the more sublime tones of this emotion. Sorrow has been replaced by anxiety and fear, for we no longer have the ability to transform our fears into sorrows. We also refuse to acknowledge our fears, and these build up over time into what we label as insecurities. Perhaps the answer to all our insecurities lies in acknowledging and addressing our fears and transforming them into sorrows. We must relearn the art of crying in solitude. In the modern world, we find ourselves driven by a happiness that is erected on competitiveness, spite, jealousy, resentment and bitterness-

A fleeting happiness that crumbles instantly.

"You can't cry when you are already empty"

Today, we define our spaces sharply…

Our house, our family, our car, our happiness.

We guard them fiercely, never letting down our defences with people. We can no longer afford to be vulnerable in an opportunistic and inhumane world. The houses that we call homes are lifeless structures filled with an emptiness that is so alien to human life. With the materialism we attach ourselves to, we also end up building layers of defence. This defence then drives our behaviour, as opposed to a bygone era when human behaviour was driven by human values- values inherent to the raw human being within us.

What have we earned with our obsession for materialism? Only defensiveness, emptiness and mental illness. The mad pursuit for materialism has reduced us to beings that have chosen to drop their consciousness to the things that really matter, for only then can we fool ourselves into believing that all is well with us and the world, and continue our pursuit for materialism.

Omid Safi writes in his column *'The disease of being busy'*[1]:

'When I ask, "How are you?" that is really what I want to know.

I am not asking how many items are on your to-do list, nor asking how many items are in your inbox. I want to know how your heart is doing, at this very moment. Tell me. Tell me your heart is joyous, tell me your heart is aching, tell me your heart is sad, tell me your heart craves a human touch. Examine your own heart, explore your soul, and then tell me something about your heart and your soul.

Tell me you remember you are still a human being, not just a human doing. Tell me you are more than just a machine, checking off items from your to-do list. Have that conversation, that glance, that touch. Be a healing conversation, one filled with grace and presence.'

The answer to all our challenges- from climate change to growing violence and mental unrest, lies in transforming our minds and our internal worlds. We must relearn the art of slow perception- a sensibility that was once natural to us. We must learn to drop our defences, feel without fear and bias, and create a new world from what we feel. We must sow the seeds for a new culture that rests on human values.

How do we connect to the raw human being within? The answer perhaps lies in the revival of literature. Literature alone can equip us with the emotional resources that are necessary to prevent a spectrum of mental illnesses unique to the pace of the modern world. In our stories, lies the answer to the integrity of our mental health. For these stories place the human mind in the context of the diversity of its environment, and explore the quest that is fundamental to every human being's journey of life:

'Who am I? What am I seeking? What is the purpose of my life?'

In essence, literature caters to the spiritual needs of a population, and in this spirituality, lies the integrity of our mental health.

Cinema is perhaps never a substitute for literature. However, there are attributes that are unique to cinema as a medium of art, making it more powerful in terms of its impact. Cinema, being a visual aesthetic experience, captures our attention more powerfully. Also, cinema being the common man's medium of art, has a greater responsibility towards sustaining the purpose of art, for it caters to a larger audience.

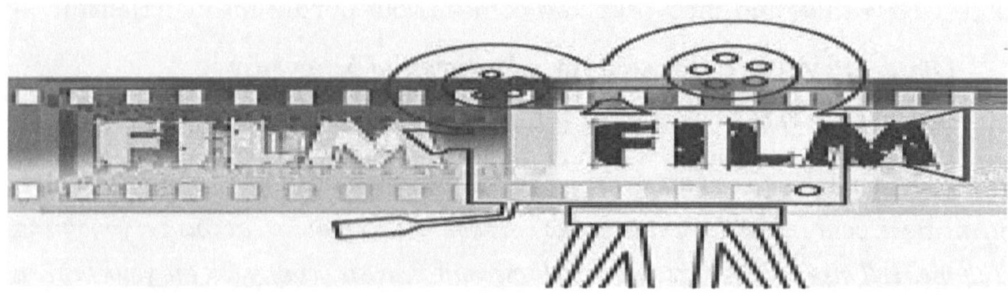

Cinema is a technologically mediated dream space. A camera has no story to tell; it requires a filmmaker to breathe life into a motion picture.

Good cinema is invariably fuelled by literature, for a story lies at the heart of good cinema. Good cinema is packed with the emotional spectrum that defines human life. It sensitizes us to the emotions that we deny ourselves in our engagements in the modern world. It bares us of the defences that refuse to accept our vulnerability in the real world and provides us the emotional engagement that is necessary to allow ourselves to feel. The experience of a good cinema helps us take a journey inward, confront our own perceptions and transform them into experiences. It helps us discover the value in these experiences. It provides us the warm companionship that is necessary to find the courage to acknowledge our vulnerability and confront our fears and sorrows.

Good cinema dispels the numbness that has taken refuge in our minds and replaces this numbness with perception.

A good cinema has layers to it. There are superficial layers that cater to the entertainment needs of the audience. But it is the core that defines good cinema. At its core, good cinema has a philosophical essence that constitutes its soul. There lies its ability to speak across time and space. It is this core that touches a chord and that we retain in some part of our unconscious as a raw, albeit profound perception that we have not perhaps decoded at that point in time. The strength of a good cinema thus lies in its ability to communicate to us at an unconscious level, for it moves us. At some point in our life, when the experience of life has permeated us enough, good cinema draws valuable inferences for us from our experiences. Our minds now learn to decode the philosophical essence hidden at the core of good cinema.

In its core, we discover the deep philosophy of life that liberates us from all our pain and suffering in the mortal world.

Good cinema counsels, providing answers to the questions we ask of our lives and teaches us the art of rising above the negativity of our circumstances. Good cinema mimics life in its infinite potential at drawing inferences. There is always a new perspective that one discovers in it; something relevant to the current climate of one's life. It makes one marvel at the infinity of essence that is packed into three hours of cinema.

In this context, ***Malayalam cinema*** has created a rich compilation of films that qualifies for good cinema. It takes us on a journey across the landscape of the human mind, exploring its infinite possibilities, sensitizing us to the immense potential that lies hidden in the abyss of the mind. It gives us a glimpse of the different shades and hues of the mind, and teaches us the art of comprehending the non-verbal language in which our minds communicate to us.

These films draw an important conclusion with reference to the human mind:

Our minds are far beyond us. The ingredients that our minds seek for sustenance are far removed from the superficial pleasures we attach ourselves to. The ultimate purpose of our lives is far beyond what we imagine the purpose of our lives to be. The motivational drives of the human mind are often deeper than what is visible on the surface and what we consciously recognize.

Malayalam cinema has attempted to explore this depth. It brings us to the realization that the integrity of our mental health lies not in fragmenting our emotions, but in sustaining them so as to reconstitute a holistic emotion that is trying to make itself visible to us. It has taught us that the science that dissects the emotional architecture of our brains can never be the guardian of our mental health. Instead, the flame of our souls is sustained by the soulful stories that exist all around us, and they alone can tide us through the darkest moments of our lives, our sanity intact.

Hidden within the philosophical core of every cinema/story, is the answer to a complexity in human life. Through the depth of our perception, we arrive at this answer.

As a student of Medicine and as a student of life, I have found that the answer to the sustenance of the human spirit, and therefore, to the mental health issues that afflict the modern world, lies not in psychotropic drugs, but in literature and cinema. The need for good cinema must therefore be recognized in a world where there is an acute need to provide resources that cater to the mental health needs of a community.

A BOOK A DAY KEEPS THE PSYCHIATRIST AWAY!

Malayalam Cinema: The Artist's Exploration Of The Human Mind

Malayalam cinema has largely been inspired by the complexity of the human mind. Its narrative has often been powered by the need to understand man's deepest motivational drives.

'What drives human behaviour?' has been the fundamental quest of most films. These films have closely looked at what motivates people and how people go about their lives, driven by these motives, rising above the negativity of the diverse circumstances that encompass human life.

When one considers the technological prowess that man has attained, it is ironical that science has made little progress in deciphering the intricacies of the human mind. The human mind remains an enigma.

Why are people different in their motivational drives? Why do people differ in their approach to a challenge? Why are some individuals more prone to mental illness? Are creativity and mental illness two sides of the same coin?

Science offers no concrete answers to these questions. As the poet rightly reflected in his verses:

'Oru shasthra granthavum innollam kandilla
manamenna prathibhasam sookshmamayi'

(To date, no scientific composition has ever been able to visualize the phenomenon of the mind with clarity)

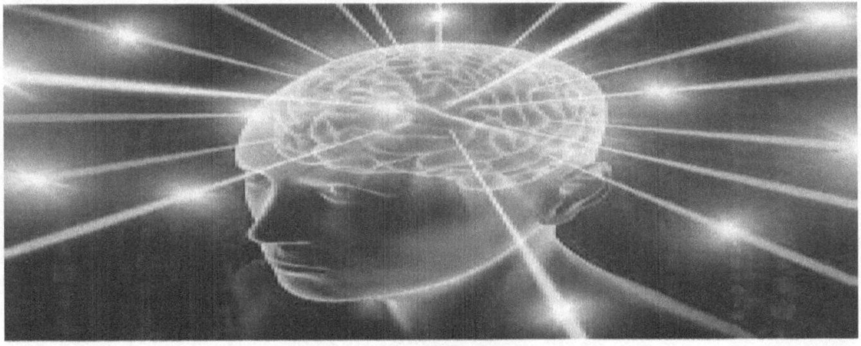

WHAT LIES BENEATH?

While science continues to devise sophisticated tools to explore the abstract of emotions, human behaviour remains the most potent tool to study the human mind. Behaviour is the only holistic, external manifestation of the human mind. In our behaviour is encoded the mystery of our minds. It is infinity that resides in the abyss of the human mind. In this network of infinity, no element can be studied in isolation for it is inseparably linked to all other components of the network. Also, this network is inseparably linked to the environment. Art preserves these invisible interconnections in the stories that explore human behaviour in the context of its environment, and thus offers valuable insights into the mind. Art alone is capable of reflecting on the deep essence of the mind, and spell it out without really spelling it. Art is therefore a more potent tool than science in shedding light on the intricacies of the human mind. Science must interconnect with art, in order to gain more insight into the emotional architecture of the brain.

"*The universe is made of stories, not of atoms.*"

- Muriel Rukeyser

The connection between literature and psychology is evident from history:

Sigmund Freud, the father of modern psychoanalysis, himself acknowledged that "the poets" discovered the unconscious before he did, stating further that the author Dostoevsky could not be understood without psychoanalysis.[2]

"Dostoevsky gives me more than any scientist, more than Gauss."

- Albert Einstein

Dostoevsky, the great 19th-century Russian author, was the son of a Muscovite doctor. His writings (The Brothers Karamazov, The Idiot, and Notes from Underground) reveal rich portrayals of psychiatric cases, including epilepsy, hysteria, dementia and psychopathy, and his psychological insights are remarkable in world literature. His characterisation of unconscious psychological motivation prefigures terms later described by the psychoanalytic movement.[2]

Fyodor Dostoyevsky, Russian writer and philosopher

Dostoevsky's novel, The Eternal Husband, appeared in 1870, when Sigmund Freud was just 14. It portrays defense mechanisms now known as repression, reaction formation, displacement and rationalisation, as well as unconscious material surfacing in dreams and impulses. Not until 1926 (Inhibitions, Symptoms and Anxiety) did Freud reformulate repression as one among many defenses, naming other mechanisms (reaction formation, displacement and rationalisation) which operate when repressed material threatens to return to consciousness.[2]

Malayalam cinema has made significant attempts at exploring the human psyche through the plot of a story. The central theme of many of these films has been portrayal of different personality types and the behaviour that is unique to each. It is therefore not surprising that a good many films have incorporated mental health themes into their storylines.

Study of the human mind must attempt to understand the multitude of climates that prevail in the mind, the external and internal factors that shape this climate, and the infinite paths through which the climate eventually manifests.

Malayalam cinema offers us a rich compilation of films that have closely studied the human mind in the context of the diversity of its environment.

Malayalam cinema has essentially portrayed mental illness as a coping mechanism of the mind in the setting of adversity. Survival is man's most potent drive. To survive, the mind may adopt any of the infinite paths available for it to overcome an obstacle in its path. Malayalam cinema has treated mental illness as one of the paths adopted by an overly sensitive mind for survival, if that is what it takes to survive. Most films have portrayed mental illness as a very natural reaction to adversity, emphasizing how human the phenomenon of mental illness is. It has therefore shaped the common man's attitude to mental illness.

"*Highly sensitive people are too often perceived as weaklings or damaged goods. To feel intensely is not a symptom of weakness; it is the trademark of the truly alive and compassionate. It is not the empath who is broken; it is society that has become dysfunctional and emotionally disabled. There is no shame in expressing your authentic feelings. Those who are at times described as being a 'hot mess' or having 'too many issues' are the very fabric of what keeps the dream alive for a more caring, humane world.***"**

- Anthon St. Maarten

Human behaviour is a spectrum. The line between sanity and insanity is thin, contrary to what we imagine. Malayalam cinema has sensitized us to how thin this line is. While modern psychiatry attempts to push more and more deviant behaviour into the label of mental illness, Malayalam cinema teaches us to probe into this deviant behaviour and embrace it as a human phenomenon that deserves empathy and understanding. These films raise an important question in our minds:

What is normal? What is the yardstick for normal? Who defines normal?

"*We do not see things as they are; we see things as we are.***"**

- Anais Nin

One is reminded of ***Nietzsche's*** words:

'Digressions, objections, delight in mockery, carefree mistrust are signs of health; everything unconditional belongs in pathology.'

Most films have refrained from romanticizing or stigmatizing mental illness. Instead, they have empathized with it. They have brought us face to face with mental illness- an entity we choose to alienate ourselves from, in the course of our unruffled lives. They have studied individuals in their social context and given us a glimpse of the delicate interplay between the mind and its environment. They have liberated our entrapped psyches by providing valuable insights into the infinite potential of the human mind.

Malayalam cinema is perhaps an example of how the most ingenious works of art are often fostered under conditions of rigid conservatism.

Kerala represents a strange concoction of cultural richness and rigid conservatism. Traditionally, the society is constructed on a rigid framework that fiercely guards its value system and sets humanely impossible ideals. The pressure to conform to a social ideal is high. The codes of conduct, morality and gender roles are rigidly defined. The lines between black and white, between right and wrong, are impossibly sharp. It is therefore not surprising that this little state has one of the highest suicide rates in the country.

The stories that formed the backbone of Malayalam cinema were thus born out of a need to rise out of this pain and suffering that was common to human life in this society. Literature and cinema played an important role in liberating the entrapped psyche of a society bound by its stories of psychological entrapment. Cinema was directed at sensitizing the common man to the potential of his mind. Cinema was a mirror that reflected his own self-worth and the value in his stories of pain and struggle, making his life bearable and worthwhile. Cinema thus aided the common man in defining the higher meaning of his life.

Kerala which is in the forefront in literacy and development, has over 30 lakh persons affected with mental disorders, according to the report by the Kerala State Mental Health Authority. This figure would amount to 10 percent of the total Kerala population.

The study reports that one in five suffer from emotional and behavioural disorders.

As per records of the Kerala Crime Records Bureau, 19 percent of suicides that happen in the state are due to mental disorders. Kerala stands second in suicide rates in the country. [3]

In an era characterized by the progressive deterioration of mental health, as evidenced by a steep rise in mental illness, there is perhaps a need to revisit the core of these films and sensitize masses to their significance from a mental health perspective. It is perhaps our moral responsibility to preserve the deep essence of these films and pass them on to the generations ahead, for these films are textbooks that capture the essence of the human psyche against the backdrop of human life.

Self-Actualization In Malayalam Cinema

A good many Malayalam films in the past have recognized that self-actualization is the ultimate goal of every human being- our master motive in this mortal life.

Self-actualization represents the ultimate level of psychological development of a human being wherein he actualizes himself as fully as possible in the real world, expressing and activating all his inherent capacities, thus realizing his full potential. Self-actualization is key to man's internal happiness and peace, for in the self-actualized state, he becomes all that he is capable of becoming.[4]

'If you plan on being anything less than you are capable of being, you will probably be unhappy all the days of your life.'

Abraham Maslow, a pioneer humanistic psychologist, described common characteristics of self-actualized individuals:

> *Every person has a strong desire to realize his or her full potential, to reach a level of self-actualization. Self-actualized individuals indicate a coherent personality syndrome and represent optimal psychological health and functioning.*

An individual enjoys peak experiences and high points in life when the individual is in harmony with himself and his surroundings.

Self-actualized individuals are reality centred and are able to differentiate what is fraudulent from what is genuine. They are also problem-centred, treating life's difficulties as problems that demand solutions. These individuals are comfortable being alone and have healthy interpersonal relationships. They generally have only a few close friends and family rather than a large number of shallow relationships.

They are spontaneous and creative, and are not bound too strictly by social conventions. They have a better insight of reality and they deeply accept themselves, others and the world. They are very independent and private with regard to their environment and culture, especially their own individual potentialities and inner resources. They experience moments of intense awareness of ecstasy, harmony and deep involvement in the world that make them feel part of a greater whole.[4]

There are many films in this category that illustrate self-actualized personalities. These films highlight the fact that this desire for self-actualization lies within each of us, forming the basis of our motivational drives.

The characters of *Ammini* in **Aranyakam**[66], *Clara* in **Thoovanathumbikal**[67], *Bhadra* in **Mazha**[68], *Balamani* in **Nandanam**[69], *Sudhakaran Nair* in **Udyanapalakan**[70], *Appu* in **Thooval Kottaram**[71], *Sreedharan* in **Sreedharante Onnam Thirumurivu**[72], *Sophia* in **Namukku Parkkan Munthiri Thoppukal**[73], *Ambili* in **Yamanam**[74] and *Manikkutty in **Sneham**[75] represent such self-actualized personalities. These films successfully define the self-actualized state through the character sketch of these individuals who represent ordinary elements of society, but who are extraordinary in their perspective of life. The individual plots of these films differ, and so do the characters. However, all these films provide us a reference for self-actualization. They highlight the fact that irrespective of our differing personalities and our differing circumstances, our happiness lies in our ability to self-actualize.

❝Within everyday ordinary people, if you look closely, you can find some extraordinary things.❞

- Joseph Badaracco

We find ourselves relating to these characters based on the individual nature of our own personality and circumstances. For some of us, the character of

Ammini in ***Aranyakam*** or *Clara* in ***Thoovanathumbikal,*** defined by their early social alienation, may be more appealing. For others, the character of *Bhadra* in ***Mazha,*** defined by her deep dedication to her profession as a doctor, may be inspirational. Some of us may deeply relate to the character of *Sudhakaran Nair* in ***Udyanapalakan*** who finds the very purpose of his life in his kinship with gardens. For some of us, the character of *Appu* in ***Thooval Kottaram*** who finds his happiness in taking upon himself the burden of the pain and struggle of his loved ones, may strike a chord.

Nearly three decades have passed since **'Thoovanathumbikal'** *was released, but the character of Clara (* **Sumalatha** *) remains vivid in the minds of Malayalees.*

Irrespective of the background circumstances, these films educate us on how our happiness lies in rising out of the pain and suffering that characterizes our lives by discovering the larger meaning of our lives. These films teach us that the key to self-actualization lies in the acceptance of our personalities and our circumstances for only then can we reduce the conflict in our minds. The characters in the above-mentioned films are able to come to terms with the tragedies in their lives on account of the meaning they derive from these roles.

Sudhakaran Nair *is able to come to terms with losing Ammu only because he accepts his vulnerability and derives contentment from his role as caretaker of gardens. He views this as the ultimate purpose of his life and therefore reconciles with the separation from Ammu.*

Ammini survives the trauma of losing both the men in her life to death. As an individual who has reconciled early with the nature of her circumstances and accepted her vulnerability, Ammini celebrates her perceptions and thoughts and creates a world out of these- a world that she captures in her writings. She therefore finds the larger meaning of her life in her engagement with her perceptions and in capturing their essence.

In a conservative society where the social structure is so rigid that it alienates those who fail to conform to its defined ideals, cinema must serve as a means of self-liberation.

These films illustrate how behaviour, that represents man's interaction with his environment, can be modified by the human thought process to achieve a desired outcome. The above-mentioned characters demonstrate how despite the negativity of their environment, they are able to affect the environment and thereby exercise some control over how it affects them. In all the above-mentioned films, the individual is portrayed as the major cause of the final outcome. Left to the impact of the environment, *Ammini's* life of social alienation or *Bhadra's* traumatic separation could have culminated in a detrimental and tragic ending. Instead, these characters demonstrate a will to rise above the negativity of their circumstances and retain a positive expectation of their environment. Their self-fulfilling prophecies work to their advantage.

While **adjustment** is more valued in conservative societies, **growth** is crucial in the successful expression of personality. These films recognize the human being's potential for growth in the setting of vulnerability and adversity, and are therefore of inspirational value. These films explore the creative potential of the human mind by portraying characters that adopt innovative paths in order to self-actualize despite the adversity that surrounds them.

The strength of these films has been in that they look at life from a humanistic perspective. The characters in these films subscribe to the **humanistic theory of personality** that regards all human beings as individuals with inherent goodness and therefore, an inherent tendency to grow towards higher levels of functioning- levels beyond mere survival.[5] In all the above films, the multiple characters are portrayed as human beings with all the imperfections that characterize human nature. Yet, they demonstrate a will to rise to a higher order of functioning. Thus, there is realism in these films. These films make us fall in love with these characters that portray the raw human being within each one of us, and that is bound by the commonality of its needs. These films teach us that at the core, the needs of all human beings are the same; we share the same hopes and fears, the same joys and sorrows.

The plot of the film ***Kakkothikkavile Appooppan Thadikal***[76] primarily focuses on a unique circumstance in a family, involving the separation of two sisters and their subsequent reunion. However, it is the freedom of spirit and the requirement for love that characterizes the personalities of the nomadic *Lakshmi (Kakkothi)* and the orphan *Murali* that draw us to the film. The film emphasizes on how the spiritual needs of all human beings, irrespective of whether they are nomads, orphans or affluent and prominent figures in society, are the same at the core.

Kakothikkavile Appooppan Thadikal: *A story that is woven around the deep bonding between the nomadic Kakkothi (**Revathi**) and the orphan Murali (**Kiran Vergis**)*

Nokkethadhoorathu Kannum Nattu[77] is yet another instance of a film that draws inspiration from the potential of the human mind. The youthful and zealous *Girlie* who refuses to submit her spirit to illness, forms the soul of the film. She chooses to live life to the fullest until her last breath, rather than confine what remains of her life to the lifelessness of a hospital.

*Nokkethadhoorathu Kannum Nattu, directed by Fazil, was **Nadia Moidu's** debut film.*

The character of *Ambili* in **Yamanam** is strongly inspirational. An invalid restricted to a wheelchair, *Ambili* derives meaning from her creative pursuits- the models and toys she designs. Her sheer acceptance of her circumstances and her psychological strength is reflected in her ability to come to terms with her brother's insensitivity to her predicament. Also, her ability to reject the wedding proposal from her neighbour, a young doctor who deeply sympathizes with her, reflects her ability to accept the equation of her life and free herself from unrealistic expectations and psychological dependence. The character of *Manikutty* in **Sneham** shares similarities with *Ambili*'s character.

Other noteworthy characters that depict self-actualization include *Raghavan Nair* (**Valsalyam**)[78], *Rameshan Nair* (**Golanthara Vartha**)[79], *Padmanabhan Nair* (**Sneham**)[75] and *Reji* (**Manasinakkare**)[80].

All the above films lack rebellion in them. They draw inspiration from personalities that rise above the labels that society confers on them. They teach us the art of setting ourselves free from the confines of these labels, by discovering the true meaning of our lives. They teach us that the answer to labelling and social prejudices lies not in violence and rebellion, but in rising above these labels by self-actualizing. For when we rebel, we are also fighting ourselves.

In this context, films that have focussed on the ***female character*** as the central character are of immense inspirational value in a traditional society where even 'woman' is a label. *Ammini in **Aranyakam**, Bhadra in **Mazha** and Clara in **Thoovanathumbikal**, illustrate* powerful female characters that rise above the labels of orphan, woman or prostitute that society confers on them. Their behaviour is not coloured by the wounds that society has inflicted on them. Instead, they retain their sensitivity to society, demonstrating the lack of rebellion in them.

> ***Ammini** retains her sensitivity to a hostile and insensitive Shylaja and demonstrates empathy and compassion when Shylaja finds herself shattered by the death of Mohan, the man she aspires to marry. Ammini silently contains her own pain and suffering and consoles Shylaja.*

> *Despite Chandran's misogynistic attitude to **Bhadra**, she demonstrates sensitivity to his emotional needs.*

> *Despite her loneliness and intense need for companionship, **Clara** retains her sensitivity to Jayakrishnan's conflict and encourages him to marry Radha.*

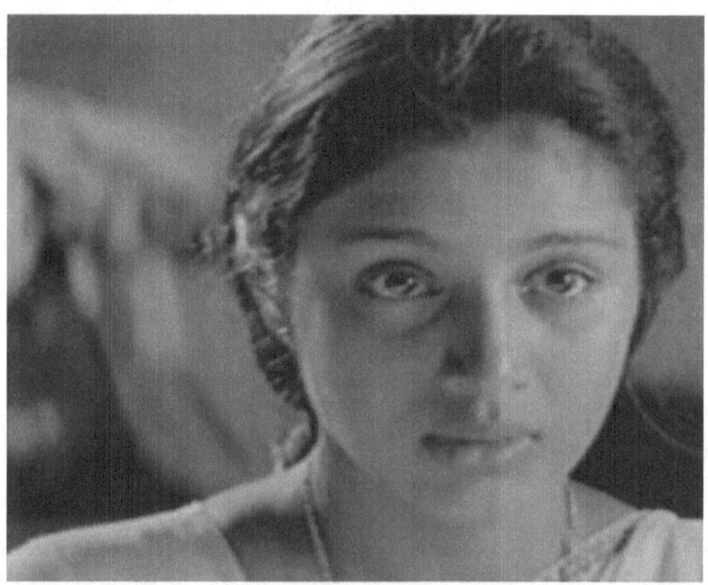

***Samyuktha Varma** in the film 'Mazha,' loosely adapted from Madhavikutty's short story '**Nashtapetta Neelambari**'*

These films teach us that the drive to surpass pain and suffering is one of the strongest drives in every human being. These films teach us to look at social labels from a different perspective; they teach us to look at them as challenges that help us activate our motivational drives and unleash our creative potential.

This discussion would probably be incomplete without adding a note on the film, *Parinayam*.[81]

Parinayam represents a sensitive study of the resilience of the human spirit in the social context of a bygone era. The film is set against the backdrop of the patriarchal oppression and confinement that characterized the lives of the *Antharjanam* (women of the *Namboodiri* community in Kerala) in the early part of the 20th centrury. This is a film of inspirational value wherein its central character, *Unnimaya Antharjanam* rises above the predicament conferred on her by her lover *Madhavan* who betrays her and by the hypocrisy of the patriarchal *Namboodiri* community that confines the life of a woman to a mere label. The film takes us through the journey of transformation of a raw, free-spirited, naïve and child-like *Unnimaya* to a mature, resilient, inspirational personality.

However, at the end of it all, one wonders if the assaults of a ruthless society on *Unnimaya* have robbed her of her free-spirited nature and transformed her into a rebel, bitter and resentful of men, on account of the wounds inflicted on her by a patriarchal society.

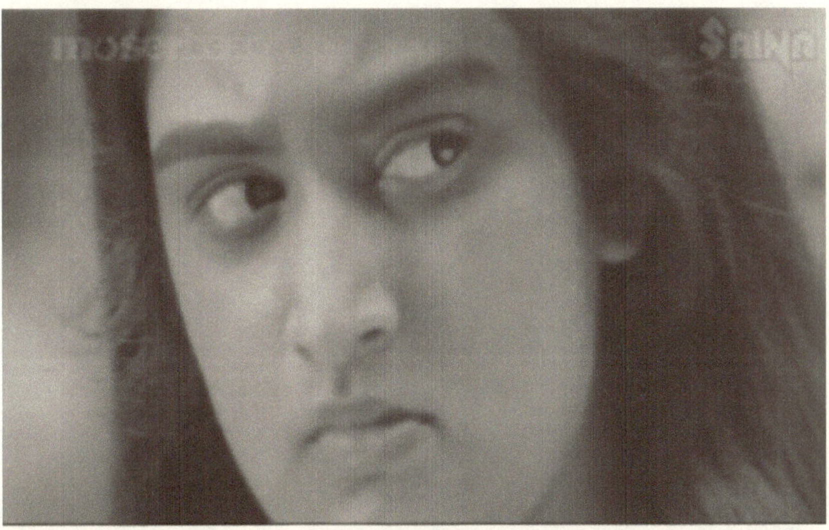

Mohini *as Unnimaya Antharjanam in the film **Parinayam** that addresses the struggle for social emancipation by women who were victims of the patriarchal oppression that characterized the Namboodiri community in Kerala in the early part of the 20th century. The film was loosely based on **Smarthavicharam** (ritualistic trial for adultery) of **Kuryeddath Thathri** in the early twentieth century that sent shockwaves across Kerala and triggered social reform movements in the community.*

It is clear from these films that resilience lies at the heart of self-actualization. These films also dispel the myth that resilience is impossible in the setting of vulnerability. All the above-mentioned characters are highly sensitive and vulnerable, and yet demonstrate resilience.

"*You never know how strong you are until being strong is the only choice you have.***"**

- Bob Marley

These films teach us to see the immense worth in our stories of vulnerability. They are pearls of wisdom in a world where our personalities are constantly striving towards expressing our genetic potential to the fullest, and where the environment is constantly striving towards shaping us into someone we are not, creating conflict. **Conflict** *lies at the root of mental illness.*

Therefore, it is the primary responsibility of cinema to focus on stories that teach us the art of reducing conflict and develop our ability at self-actualization in the diversity of circumstances that encompass human life.

"*It is not the strongest of the species that survive, nor the most intelligent, but the one most responsive to change.***"**

- Charles Darwin

The Psychological Exploration Of Aggressive Behaviour In Malayalam Cinema

"All aggression is rooted in the psychological assaults one has endured from society."

A good many Malayalam films have explored human behaviour in the light of the ***psychological defense mechanisms*** that the human mind activates in order to reduce the anxiety created by conflict. This behaviour can be examined in the light of ***Sigmund Freud's theory on personality***.

Freud postulated that personality consists of three distinct, but interacting parts- the id, the ego and the super ego.

*The **id** is the raw, unorganized, inherited part of personality, concerned with the immediate gratification of the instinctual needs. It is completely selfish for it blindly seeks gratification.*

However, reality prevents the demands of the id from being fulfilled in most cases. This causes conflict, and therefore anxiety.

*The **ego** is the outgrowth of the id formed to direct an individual's impulses in accordance with reality. It provides a buffer between the id and reality. It makes use of reason and other intellectual and cognitive resources in order to deal with the external world, while simultaneously exercising some control over the id's demands. Thus, ego is the executive of personality and it helps integrate the individual into society.*

*The **super ego** represents the values of society handed down by an individual's parents, teachers and other important figures. The individual adopts rules, restrictions and conducts of behaviour based on what is fed into his life from these figures.*

Thus, the id, ego and super ego continuously interact and direct our behaviour, largely at an unconscious level.[6,7]

__Defense mechanisms__ represent the unconscious mechanisms that an individual develops in the setting of conflict. These are directed by the ego in order to reduce the anxiety created by the conflict between the id and reality. As long as they do *not interfere with our ability to cope realistically with problems, they represent a normal human reaction. The objective of these defense mechanisms is to safeguard the integrity and worth of the self.*

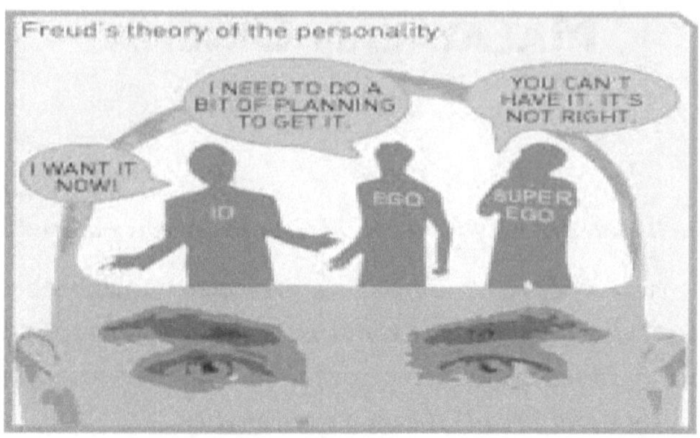

Defense mechanisms include denial, repression, suppression, projection, rationalization, dissociation, reaction formation and displacement.[8,9]

The characters discussed in the previous chapter are characterized by **acceptance** of conflict and therefore the activation of **mature defense mechanisms** such as humour, sublimation, suppression, altruism and anticipation in order to deal with conflict. These defense mechanisms do not interfere with the process of self-actualization, for they successfully overcome the denial that is one's natural, primary reaction to stress, thus integrating the individual in a healthy manner into the scheme of reality.[10,11]

However, deviant behaviour and mental illness is rooted in the phenomenon of **denial**.

*The theory of denial was first researched seriously by **Anna Freud**. She classified denial as a mechanism of the immature mind, because it conflicts with the ability to learn from and cope with reality.*[8]

*Many contemporary psychoanalysts treat denial as the first stage of a coping cycle. When an unwelcome change occurs, a trauma of some sort, the process of coping begins with a disbelief and denial towards the trauma. That **denial**, in a healthy mind, slowly rises to greater consciousness. Gradually becoming a subconscious pressure, just beneath the surface of overt awareness, the mechanism of coping then involves a temporary **repression**, while the person accumulates the emotional resources to fully face the trauma. The person then deals with the trauma in a stage alternately called **acceptance**, depending on* *the scope of the issue and the therapist's school of thought. Once sufficiently dealt with, the trauma must sink away from total conscious awareness again. Left metaphorically upon a back burner or put away in a cupboard, the subsequent process of **sublimation** involves a balance of neither quite forgetting nor quite remembering. With sublimation may begin the full resolution process, where the trauma finally sinks away into eventual forgetfulness.[8,9]*

The characters of *Sharadammini* in **Chakoram**[82] and *Bhanu* in **Kanmadam**[83] are sensitive illustrations of **immature defense mechanisms** that represent persistent **denial** and that take the shape of aggression. **Aggression** dominates the character sketch of both these female personalities who are forced into a caretaker role early in their lives. *Sharadammini* adopts the role of a parent early in her life and tends to the needs of her siblings while they remain insensitive to her emotional needs and ungrateful to her contribution to their lives. Unlike *Sudhakaran Nair's* personality in **Udyanapalakan**, *Sharadammini* is not in acceptance of this equation of her life. Her inability to come to terms with this equation (*denial*) lies at the root of her eccentric behaviour. She is in denial of her deep sensitivity and vulnerability, and this denial manifests as the irrational anger, vigilance and resentment that she expresses to society in general. In reality, the anger conceals her sorrow and disappointment over the equation of her life, and thus protects her fragile self-esteem, which is of utmost importance to her. She prefers to conceal her vulnerability and deep longing for love, affection and care, and instead directs this negative psychic energy into her anger.

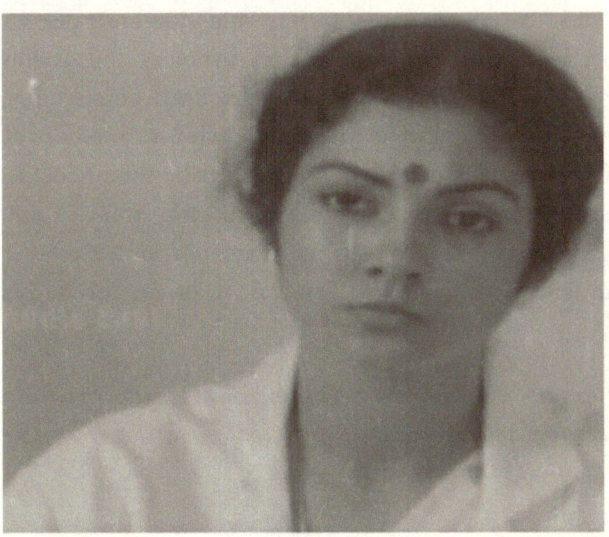

Shanthi Krishna in 'Chakoram,' a story of unrequited love

Anger is a normal emotion that we all have. Healthy anger gives people the momentum to produce necessary change. Anger, appropriately used, can create social change. Healthy anger can be constructive in making a difference to a situation. However, unhealthy and inappropriate anger poses problems both to the individual and to society.

Anger can be substituted when one feels guilty and cannot own up to an act. Anger can be substituted to avoid the more painful feelings of embarrassment and humiliation.

Anger can be used to shut down the internal unpleasant feelings of vulnerability and helplessness, as anger is a more comfortable emotion to feel. Anger can also be used to intimidate and force the other person to back off and stop their criticism.

Anger then becomes the prevalent emotion used to avoid pain. The habit of shielding oneself with the anger defense becomes a learned behaviour of self-protection. Anger becomes entrenched as a protective device and one has trouble giving it up. [12,13]

Sharadammini therefore adopts anger as an unconscious defense mechanism despite the fact that it is not an element of her fundamental nature. Deep within, she resents her own behaviour, but feels compelled to adopt it in order to internalize the unpleasant equation of her life and protect her fragile self-esteem.

Sharadammini **projects** her emotions onto society. She maintains a critical and judgmental attitude towards society and demonstrates a tendency to blame, irrespective of the true nature of circumstances. This is illustrated in her reaction to her maid *Ammini Amma*, her *Ammavan* (uncle), her neighbours, her subordinates at work, and all the people who form a part of her day-to-day life. Her behaviour is persistently governed by the prejudiced perception that society sees through her vulnerability and looks at it as a weakness that is meant to be exploited. She projects her perception of her own self to society. She therefore detests vulnerability as a trait in others for it mirrors her own vulnerability.

Projections are a defensive mechanism where we ignore what we do not like about ourselves and become upset about that same trait in another. They are the disowned aspect of our personality.

Projections protect us by keeping a lid on the terror that knowledge of our negative qualities might provoke. One projects one's own guilt and anger on to others when one judges and labels the other person's actions instead of just observing or witnessing them. Carl Jung believed that the projection defense functions like a mirror between the ego and the id. The negative characteristic that has been disowned which has been tying up psychic energy in the ego will be reflected in the person's daily experience.

What we resist, persists. Projections are warning signals that something is unresolved in oneself.[8,9]

The character sketch of *Bhanu* in **Kanmadam** is closely aligned to the character of *Sharadammini*. The strength of these films lies in that they empathise with these characters and illuminate the significance of sensitivity in our interactions with people. They expose the vulnerability of these characters beneath their layers of defense and reflect their immense need for love and their ability to love. These films take us on a realistic journey through the lives and minds of these individuals.

Manju Warrier gets into the skin of the rebellious character 'Bhanu' in Kanmadam.

One is reminded of verses from the poem *'Please hear what I am not saying,'* by *Charles Finn*:

"Don't be fooled by me.
Don't be fooled by the face I wear
for I wear a mask, a thousand masks,
masks that I'm afraid to take off,
and none of them is me.

Sargam[84] is yet another film that comes to mind in the context of aggression as the reflection of a defense mechanism. The character of *Kuttan Thampuran* is characterized by his aggression that is born out of the negative circumstances of his childhood, chiefly the lack of a protective paternal influence. Also, his epileptic seizures draw much ridicule and humiliation from his friends at school, and his aggression is rooted in this humiliation and his denial of the equation of his life. While aggression dominates his behaviour, the film takes us through moments that expose his deep affection for his childhood companion *Haridas*, exposing the sensitivity that lies at the core of his personality. This sensitivity is also manifest in the tragic ending to his life wherein he commits suicide upon the realization that his marriage is constructed on *Haridas's* sacrifice of his love.

Kuttan Thampuran (Sargam): The character that established *Manoj K Jayan's* proficiency as an actor

A comparison of the above films also illustrates how denial as a defense mechanism is stronger in males, as opposed to females, manifesting as strong aggression that is directed to significant social and self harm.

The character of *Sally* in **Desatanakkilli Karayarilla**[85] is another character that comes to mind in the context of aggression. *Sally's* outrageous reaction and general hostility to society is a reflection of her defense. This is discussed in detail in the chapter on gender conflict.

Jealousy that manifests as aggression also represents denial. The character of *Ramanathan* in **Bharatham**[86] portrays jealousy as the reflection of a defense mechanism. *Ramanathan*, an acclaimed Carnatic music vocalist, feels threatened by the rising fame of his younger brother, *Gopinathan* whom he deeply loves. He is torn between the unpleasant feelings that develop in him in response to his devaluation as an acclaimed musician and the love that he harbours for his younger brother. This reflects the deep meaning he derives from both his roles- his role as a musician, and his role as an elder brother. When his role as a musician is no longer valued, he feels insecure and directs this insecurity to *Gopinathan*, who has taken his place. His conflict compels him to step out of both his roles and abscond.

Jealousy is actually a biological defense mechanism used to react to a perceived threat to a valued relationship wherein one is afraid of losing something of meaning. Instinctively, people become defensive in order to protect the value of their commitment to another person or situation.[14]

Nedumudi Venu *as Ramanathan in* **Bharatham**, *a film that is viewed as a modern-day adaptation of the Ramayana. The film won three national awards.*

Apart from the films mentioned here, there are many other films that have successfully portrayed the aggression rooted in denial, on minor and major terms. *Kunjukunjamma Thomas* in **Nokkethadoorathu Kannum Nattu**[77] portrays a mild and benign version of such defense in her outrageous approach to society while *Michael's* defense in **Oru Maravathoor Kanavu**[87] culminates in a deep tragedy.

The discussion in this chapter would be incomplete without a note on the film **Kireedam**[88], a powerful film that explores the influence of persistent conflict on the human psyche. *Sethumadhavan*, the central character of this film, is a deeply sensitive individual who aspires to be a police inspector. However, he harbours in his mind a deep fear of physical violence. This is evident in his reaction when he visits the police station to have a word with his father, and witnesses a criminal being physically abused by the policemen. Though the violence he witnesses is mild, he demonstrates an irrational fear to this display of violence. This fear represents his vulnerability that is in denial of the unpleasant feelings triggered by displays of violence.

This conflict in his mind assumes significance when he witnesses his father (whom he deeply loves and respects) being beaten up by the street rowdy, *Keerikkadan Jose*. The intensity of his unpleasant feelings (that he has never come to terms with) compels him to resist the reality he witnesses and this resistance drives him to react violently to *Jose*. This impulsive violence demonstrated by *Sethumadhavan* contrasts with his fundamental peace loving, docile, non-violent nature.

Thus, the plot skilfully demonstrates how denial can cause us to act against our basic nature.

Mohanlal *won the 1989 National Film Award-Special Jury Award for his role in* **Kireedam.**

The film subsequently takes us through a series of circumstances wherein *Sethumadhavan* is progressively thrust into such defensive violence. The conflict in his mind rises progressively as he realizes that his behaviour is opposed to his emotional values. The situation eventually gets out of hand as he is repeatedly provoked into defense. The severity of the conflict in his mind and the intense anxiety aroused is reflected in the climax, wherein he brutally kills *Jose*, and demonstrates severe aggression. He appears dissociated from reality as an outcome of the severe conflict and anxiety.

In this regard, the film shares similarity with **Thaniyavarthanam**[89], wherein *Balan* persistently fights the label of insanity that society confers on him and the denial of this equation eventually culminates in deep anxiety and a tragic ending.

All these films take us through the phenomenon of denial, and therefore, unresolved conflict that takes the shape of aggression, hostility, jealousy or resentment. They explore deviant behaviour that largely remains within the domains of sanity, but builds into a perpetual cycle of mental unrest. They emphasize the role of acceptance and healthy defense mechanisms in the context of the integrity of our mental health.

Conflict Of Identity In Malayalam Cinema

A few Malayalam films have studied the influence of social norms, beliefs and values in the development of personality. Films that come to the mind in this context are **Vadakkunokkiyantram**[90], **Pavam Pavam Rajakumaran**[91] and **Chinthavishtayaya Shyamala**[92]. The central theme of all these films is denial to an aspect of the self that conflicts with the value system defined by contemporary society.

> *The 'self' is a central theme in psychology. It attempts to define who we really are, beneath all the roles we play. William James classified the self into:*
>
> - *The **material self**, referring to the body and its possessions*
> - ***Social self**, referring to the social roles we play*
> - ***Spiritual self**, referring to our cognitions*
> - ***Pure ego**, referring to our identity*
> - ***The central active self***
>
> *The central active self is the true essence of an individual, and remains relatively constant. It controls and integrates all the other selves.*
>
> *Pure ego represents our identity or self-concept in terms of who we see ourselves as– our concept of our material, social and spiritual selves.*
>
> *The **ideal self** refers to what one would like to be. The extent to which the self-concept and ideal self differ is an indicator of discomfort, dissatisfaction and neurotic difficulties. Accepting oneself as one actually is, and not as one wishes to be, is a sign of mental health.[15,16]*

The plot of **Vadakkunokkiyantram** is set against the backdrop of a conventional society that attributes overt significance to physical attributes such as complexion and stature as indices of social acceptance. The central character of this film, *Thalathil Dineshan, is* a sensitive individual who is in denial of his short stature and dark complexion for these attributes conflict with the value system of contemporary society. *Dineshan's* ego perceives these attributes as unappealing and distasteful- beliefs shaped by society.

He therefore lives in denial of his material self and his behaviour is constantly driven by this denial. His eccentricity is rooted in this denial. He displays an obsessive engagement with his body image- he powders his face obsessively, spends hours in front of the mirror, and writes endlessly to columnists for remedies to his dark complexion.

Sreenivasan as the eccentric 'Dineshan' in **Vadakkunokkiyantram**

This denial takes a new dimension when he gets married to *Shobha*, a beautiful woman by social standards. The conflict in his mind grows and transforms into a constant **obsession** for he believes that he is not a good match for *Shobha*. He fears that other men might take advantage of this equation. He views reality through a cloud of insecurity rooted in his denial.

Dineshan (Sreenivasan) believes that he is not a good match for **Shobha (Parvathy).**

He is in constant suspicion of all the men he encounters- the bachelors in his neighbourhood, the men who are seated next to *Shobha* at the cinema theatre when he takes her out for a movie, the men who have scribbled poems in her autograph book, and all the men she interacts with, including his own brother. He reflects on their behaviour obsessively and reads into them illogically. This obsessive thought process that tries to analyze situations through the lens of his insecurity begins to take the shape of ***delusions*** that become serious enough to cause harm to his near and dear ones. The conflict in his mind progressively increases and eventually culminates in his admission to a mental asylum. He is then treated and counselled by a psychiatrist who educates him on the roots of his eccentric behaviour. The insight into the problem changes his perspective and he returns to begin life afresh.

The climax is the strength of the film. A cured *Dineshan* wakes up in the middle of the night, vigilant and suspicious, certain that there is an intruder in the premises of his house. The film conveys how human behaviour is largely a matter of habit. *Dineshan*'s eccentric behaviour is chronic and the chronicity makes it difficult for him to shed it off completely, despite the awareness of its source and origin. It reflects on how the self-concept, once formed, tends to defend and maintain itself.

A vigilant and suspicious Dineshan in the climax of ***Vadakkunokkiyantram***

The film also addresses the psychological need of individuals for a *positive regard* from others- the universal requirement to be loved and respected. It illustrates how we compare the values of others with our self-concept. The psychological consequences depend on the discrepancy between these. If the discrepancy is great, the conflict and anxiety is significant.

The self desperately needs and seeks acceptance, love, warmth, care and reassurance from others. It is vulnerable. It is this need for positive regard that makes a person ignore inner signals and act in a manner that fetches approval and support. So strong is this need for positive regard that it can cause individuals to act contrary to what they feel is right.

The rules, regulations or guides for behaviour imposed on us by others as a condition for their positive regard are called conditions of worth. Such conditions of worth are the basic obstacles to accurate perception and realistic awareness. Individuals with excessively rigid and strict conditions of worth or narrowly defined self-concepts are particularly prone to distortion and denial of their experiences.[17,18]

The film thus educates us on how the value system defined by a society can influence the self-concept of an individual and be detrimental, sometimes to the point of leading them to mental illness. It also emphasizes the role of parents and society on the seeding of beliefs in children.

Pavam Pavam Rajakumaran emphasizes predominantly on an individual's need for *positive regard*.

Gopalakrishnan, a teacher in a parallel college, is the object of ridicule amongst his students and peers, on account of his eccentric behaviour. *Gopalakrishnan* is portrayed as a man who has been looking for a suitable match for ages, but ends up facing constant rejection. *Gopalakrishnan's* aspirations in terms of a suitable match are unrealistic in that there is tremendous discrepancy between his self-concept and his ideal self. He constantly attempts to project himself as the 'ideal self,' but people see through this. This makes him desperate as he fails to find a match.

It is the desperate need for positive regard that drives him to fall into the trap set up by his friends. *Gopalakrishnan* finds himself obsessively pursuing a woman who he believes is madly in love with him. As the obsession increases, he goes to great lengths to materialize his dream of marrying her.

*Sreenivasan as the obsessive 'Gopalakrishnan' and **Rekha** as 'Radhika'- the object of his obsession, in **Pavam Pavam Rajakumaran***

The miserly *Gopalakrishnan* transforms into an individual who spends thoughtlessly under the influence of his obsession. *Gopalakrishnan* demonstrates impulsive behaviour and progressively detaches from the reality of his life. He neglects his social roles and responsibilities and chases *Radhika*, the 'love of his life.' He follows her and confronts her. He refuses to believe her when she denies knowledge of the events that he describes with regard to the past interactions between the two of them. He ends up making a nuisance of himself and the obsession culminates in dire conflict when he is beaten up by the public for harassing the woman.

It takes such a big setback to eventually pull *Gopalakrishnan* out of his obsession and come to terms with reality. *Gopalakrishnan* finally learns of the trick played by his friends, and he comes to acceptance.

Acceptance transforms him as an individual for he abandons the concept of the ideal self he has harboured all along and learns to accept himself as he is. He also learns that it can be detrimental to persistently look outside of oneself for positive regard. He now becomes self-reliant. The film ends on a happy note, with *Gopalakrishnan* marrying the very woman who had been the object of his obsession. The climax portrays a transformed *Gopalakrishnan*, self-actualized and free from defense and denial, his behaviour consistent with his self-concept.

The film therefore educates us on how acceptance and learning can transform us in a healthy direction.

Chinthavishtayaya Shyamala differs from the above films in that it portrays a character who is in ***denial of the social self.*** The central character of this film, *Vijayan*, demonstrates a denial to all his social roles- that of a spouse, father and breadwinner. His identity feeds off the belief that he is not capable of taking on these roles and responsibilities. However, the social values conflict with this identity for they define a man as the breadwinner of his family and as one shouldering the responsibilities of the spouse and children.

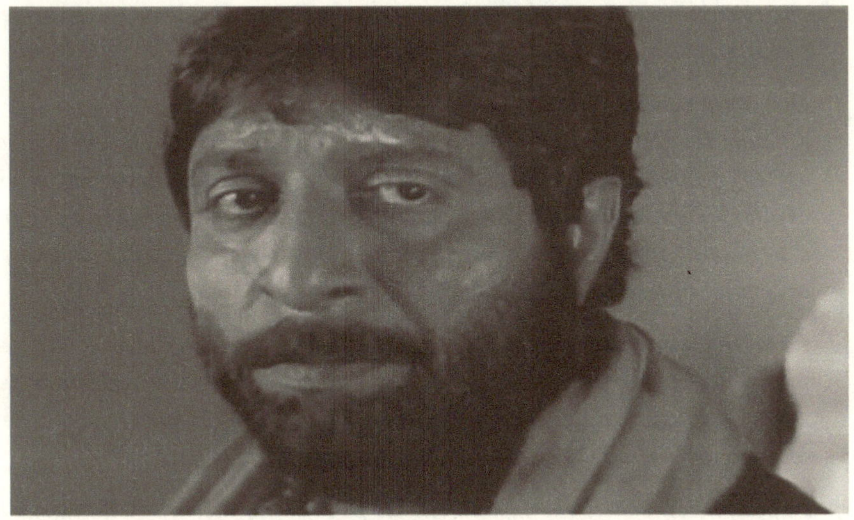

Sreenivasan plays the escapist 'Vijayan' in ***Chinthavishtayaya Shyamala***

Vijayan demonstrates ***avoidance*** towards all the situations that demand these roles. He absents himself from work, pursuing unrealistic business ventures that fail miserably. He also avoids confrontations with his wife and father and resorts to escapism. His father makes numerous attempts to reform him, but they all fail. Eventually, his father compels him to take up the pilgrimage at *Sabarimala*, observing the customary forty one day fasting and abstinence. *Vijayan* discovers in this act a new outlet for his escapism. He embraces the garb of an ascetic, and takes to an *Ashram*, believing this to be the perfect answer to his inability to fit into his social role. However, he soon discovers that he is unable to conform to the true role of an ascetic. He realizes that the source of the conflict is his own personality, and not the circumstances that surround him. With this realization, he goes back home and the rest of the film takes us through his struggle to get back into his social role as a spouse, father and breadwinner. Yet again, this film enlightens us on how denial can alienate us from society and prevent us from leading a healthy life. *Vijayan* demonstrates eventually that it is possible for him to carry out his social roles, but it is the denial that has prevented him from even making attempts at taking on these roles.

> *The **social cognitive theory** views the self as an outcome of social learning and cognition. Thus, behaviour is not a passive phenomenon that represents the outcome of circumstances. It is an active phenomenon, wherein our cognition and the ability to learn, also govern the final outcome. It is strongly influenced by our competencies, encoding strategies and expectancies.*[19,20]

> *Our **competencies** refer to our ability to use information actively in order to generate thoughts and actions that are capable of modifying the influence of our environment on us. Our ability to take the initiative and effort to use available information and thus confront the challenges in life is an important determinant of the final outcome. A passive approach to the environment can thus make us victims of the environment.*[21]

> ***Encoding strategies*** *refer to the attributes that we focus on, when confronted with a challenge. In confronting a challenge, we must take into consideration our strengths as much as our weaknesses. If we selectively focus on our weaknesses, we are more likely to be in denial, and also more likely to fail.*[21]

> ***Expectancies*** *refer to the expectation we have of our actions. If we expect to succeed, we are more likely to attempt with sincerity and effort. If we expect to fail, we are likely to demonstrate denial and avoidance.*[21]

Through the characters of Dineshan, Gopalakrishnan and Vijayan, the above-mentioned films enlighten us on how denial of the self is often the outcome of poor competencies, faulty encoding strategies and negative expectancies. The films do not explore in detail the factors that are responsible for these attributes of personality, but they draw important conclusions on how the resultant denial of the self can interfere seriously with leading a healthy social life. They also stress on the importance of cognition and learning in the development of personality.

"Unless we base our sense of identity upon the truth of who we are, it is impossible to attain true happiness."

- Brenda Shoshanna

GENDER CONFLICT IN MALAYALAM CINEMA

Desatanakkili Karayarilla[85], written and directed by **P.Padmarajan**, was a film far ahead of its times. The film was an insightful study of human behaviour in a social context from multiple perspectives. It made its mark in that it studied a unique facet of deviant behaviour- that of gender conflict.

The film explores the personality of two female characters, *Sally* and *Nimmi*, who represent outcomes of a shattered childhood. It dwells on how our personalities are the outcome of our past experiences, particularly our early childhood experiences.

The film reflects on the role of parental love, security and protection in the normal mental development of a child.

P. Padmarajan: A director far ahead of his times. He was noted for his fine and detailed screenwriting, expressive direction style and his astute portrayal of human relationships and emotions. (Reproduced with permission from Team Indulekha: http://indulekha.com/moviegallery/2006/02/padmarajan.html)

Sally and *Nimmi* are two adolescent girls studying in a boarding school. Despite their strikingly different personalities, they are bound into a deep-rooted relationship by the commonality of their individual circumstances. They are both victims of parental disharmony. While their parents are divorced and have moved on with their lives, the two girls are brought up in a negative environment where they find themselves surrounded by unhappiness, frustration, loneliness, hopelessness and hostility. Apart from the things money can buy, there is nothing positive in their environment.

The common emotional void in their lives forms the foundation for their inseparable relationship.

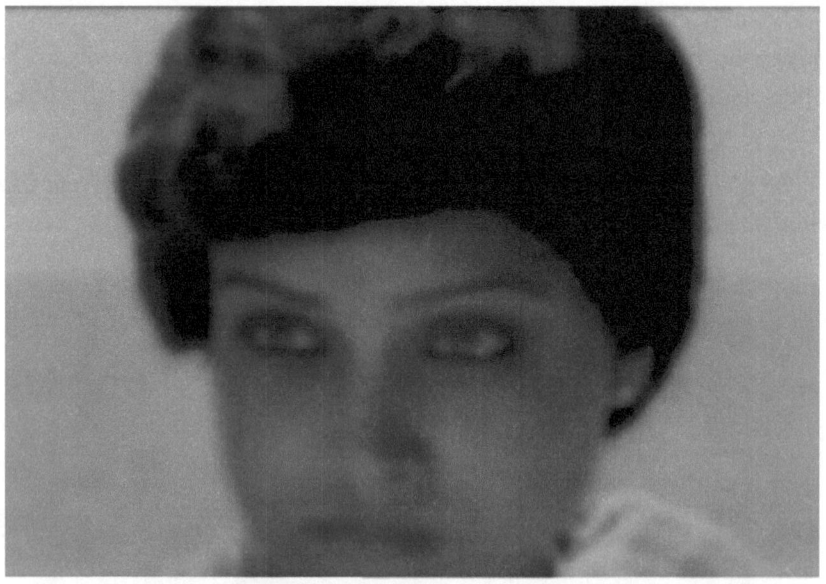

*Shaari was introduced to Malayalam Cinema by Padmarajan. She played the lead character in his film, **Namukku Parkkan Munthiri Thoppukal**. Shaari plays the rebellious **Sally** in **Desatanakkilli Karayarilla**.*

Sally and *Nimmi* are portrayed as individuals who are incapable of developing trust in their relationship with others. They regard others with suspicion and fear, perceiving the world as a rather unsafe place. They are therefore unable to form healthy interpersonal relationships with people. They live a life of rebellion, expressing resentment towards their peers and teachers, scorning the discipline and codes of conduct laid down by their Catholic institution, finding pleasure in mischief and pranks directed at the teachers and the institution.

This rebellion represents their denial towards the trauma inflicted on their minds by their circumstances.

> **Trust** *is developed in the first year of life. When the needs of an infant are met appropriately and the infant receives genuine affection, cuddling and fondling, the infant develops a trust towards the world and perceives the world as a safe and dependable place. If the experiences are chaotic, unpredictable and rejecting, children approach the world with fear and suspicion- a behaviour that is not resolved once and for all.*[22,23]

Sally is portrayed as extremely tomboyish in her attitude, mannerisms and preferences. She is fiercely independent, strong, active, assertive, aggressive, rational and detached. Her character portrays strong masculinity. *Sally's* strong masculinity represents a denial towards her gender role.

Sally's only weakness is the soft and vulnerable *Nimmi*, towards whom she is highly protective. *Nimmi's* character is representative of strong feminine traits. She is warm, caring, submissive, dependent, tender and emotionally vulnerable. Emotional vulnerability lies at the heart of *Nimmi's* personality, and she therefore demonstrates overt dependence on *Sally*.

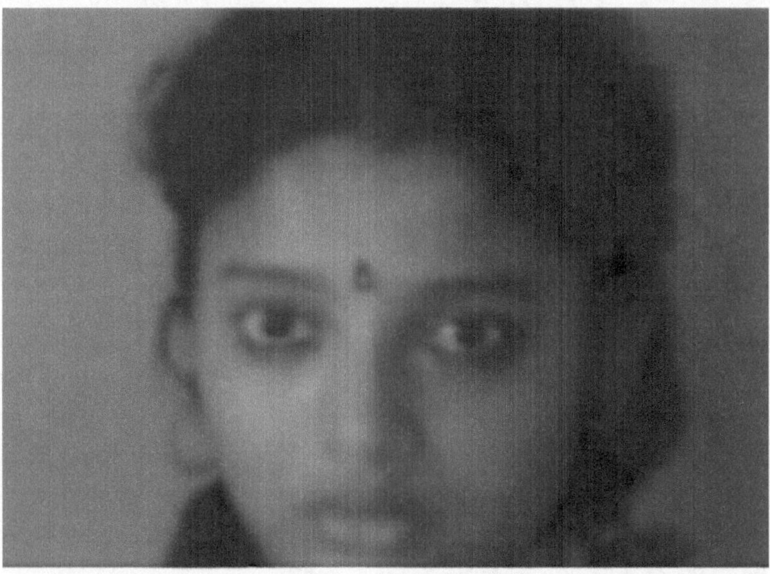

*Karthika's career as an actress in the Malayalam film industry was limited to the 80s. She was recognized for her portrayal of vulnerable, unconventional characters. In **Desatanakkilli Karayarilla**, she portrays the vulnerable **Nimmi**.*

Every society differentiates individuals as men and women on the basis of anatomical differences. Such differentiation does not stop just with anatomical aspects. It leads to assigning gender roles.

Gender identity *refers to the conceptions that people have of themselves as being male or female. From early years, children realize that they belong to a particular gender.*[24]

Gender role *refers to a set of cultural expectations that defines the way in which the members of each sex should behave. There are three recognized gender roles- masculine, feminine and androgynous.*[24]

Most people have gender identities that are consistent with the gender role standards of their society.

The film clearly illustrates a case of ***denial to gender role***, but does not draw any definite conclusion on denial to gender identity. It is left to the viewer to interpret whether *Sally* perceives herself as a male (denial to gender identity) or merely rebels against social expectations in terms of gender role (denial to gender role).

The film sheds light on the factors that culminate in gender role conflict:

Sally is raised by her mother while her father has moved on with his life following the divorce. In the absence of a father figure, *Sally* develops masculine traits that enable her to adapt to her negative circumstances. She rejects the feminine traits that she may have seen in her mother- the helplessness and dependence that have made her mother a victim of her circumstances. As a child, *Sally* may have abhorred the gender role of a female for she associates feminine traits with a negative outcome.

On the contrary, *Nimmi* is brought up by her father and her stepmother. The strong feminine traits in her personality may represent submissiveness to a strong and restricting father figure, leading to acceptance of the gender role defined by society, and may also reflect the deep emotional void and vulnerability generated by the absence of a mother figure catering to her need for love and affection. *Nimmi* therefore grows up to be a dependent personality who demonstrates passivism towards circumstances.

Autonomy *and initiative develop in a child between the ages of 2 to 5 years. As children begin to explore the world, overt protection or excessive restriction by the parents can lead to an excessive sense of shame and guilt in the child and* *a lack of confidence to take initiative. Such children grow up into vulnerable and dependent adults who become passive recipients of their environment.*[25,26]

The film dwells on how contemporary society labels these two characters on account of their deviant behaviour, failing to see beneath the external facets of their rebellious personality. The perspective of their class teacher, **Devika**, represents the perspective of contemporary society towards such deviant behaviour.

Devika is an individual who has struggled and come up the hard way. Her upbringing has taught her to value the hardships and struggle that characterize poverty, but she fails to understand the emotional emptiness that has driven *Sally* and *Nimmi* towards rebellion. Consequently, her reaction to their behaviour is criticism and punishment. She expresses hostility towards them because she fails to see beneath their rebellious personalities the scars that have been inflicted on their minds by their broken childhood. The insensitivity that society demonstrates towards these rebels drives them towards further rebellion.

The antagonism between *Devika* and the two girls eventually culminates in *Sally* and *Nimmi* eloping from school, in the setting of a picnic. The girls celebrate the news of *Devika*'s suspension over this incident.

*Urvashi is known for her versatility as an actress. In **Desatanakkilli Karayarilla**, she plays the authoritarian class teacher, **Devika**.*

The story takes a turn with the entry of **Harisankar** into their lives. *Harisankar* transforms from a stranger and acquaintance to a close companion.

His personality fills the emotional void in *Nimmi's* life. His presence makes her feel loved, protected and secure. *Nimmi's* vulnerability attaches to the care and concern he demonstrates towards her. Her fragile self-esteem finds strength in his positive regard and her deep rooted feelings of worthlessness and lack of meaning in life are put to rest. In his companionship, she discovers the answer to her quest for emotional fulfilment. She develops overt emotional dependence on him and begins to find the very meaning of her life in this companionship.

The Padmarajan-Mohanlal partnership was known for its unconventional themes. ***Mohanlal*** *plays 'Harisankar' in* ***Desatanakkilli Karayarilla***.

However, *Harisankar* is unaware of the intensity of *Nimmi's* emotions for him. He does not take her obsession towards him very seriously. He looks at it as a transient infatuation that is likely to abate in due course of time. He is totally ignorant of her dependence. Just as *Harisankar's* companionship gives *Nimmi* the courage to set right her life and come out of a life of social escapism, *Harisankar* expresses his intention of marrying *Devika*. *Nimmi's* feminine vulnerability and dependence fail to come to acceptance of this fact. *Nimmi* feels lost and fails to focus on the challenge and take an active step in confronting it. Instead, she slips into a passive state of depression. She lacks the emotional or cognitive resources that are necessary to overcome the acute trauma caused to her mind and continues to be in a state of denial and shock.

Sally, on the contrary, refuses to give in to the circumstances that put pressure on the girls to return to the life they had run away from, and makes plans to move on to a new place.

The film successfully compares the adaptive value of feminine and masculine traits in the setting of adversity and their role in the final outcome.

Though feminine gender role is adaptive in some situations, it is also associated with psychological states such as depression. It is stated that people with traditionally masculine gender roles (both men and women) experience less psychological problems like anxiety and depression than those with feminine gender roles. The passive and contemplating nature of feminine gender roles may account for excessive self-focussing and the generation of negative feelings. Such characters are dependent and may feel a lack of control in life. As a result, when they experience a problem, they focus on their helplessness which in turn may lead to negative feelings.

On the contrary, people with masculine gender roles are known to engage the least in self-focussing and experience lesser negative feelings. Their qualities of action orientation and assertiveness help in handling situations better. This gives them a sense of control and competence. Hence they focus on exploring the ways of solving a problem.[27,28]

Though *Sally*'s masculine gender role is adaptive in this situation, she gives in to her emotional commitment to *Nimmi*. She acts against her fundamental nature that values rationality and assertiveness, and commits to *Nimmi*. The film therefore draws the viewer's attention to the depth and nature of the relationship between *Sally* and *Nimmi*.

The film raises an important question: What is the true nature of the relationship between Sally and Nimmi?

The nature of the relationship between *Sally* and *Nimmi* is an important aspect of the film, considering that gender roles play a crucial role in the affinity that draws two people into a relationship. Was the relationship between *Sally* and *Nimmi* mere friendship, or was there more to it? This is a question that the film strongly raises. The answer is left to the viewer's interpretation.

All through the film, there are dialogues and responses on *Sally's* part that indicate a subtle homosexual orientation. *Padmarajan* perhaps gives an emotional dimension to homosexuality, and therefore, it is difficult to establish the true nature of *Sally's* feelings towards *Nimmi*, especially concerning sexuality. There are multiple cues throughout the film that are suggestive of *Sally's* homosexual orientation, but *Padmarajan* refrains from drawing strong conclusions and leaves it to the interpretation of the viewer.

Sally's statement to *Nimmi* when she falls in love with *Harisankar*, stating that *Nimmi* is fortunate in that she is able to fall in love and therefore escape the clutches of the past, could reflect *Sally's* inability to fall in love on heterosexual terms. The song sequences wherein *Sally* and *Nimmi* explore their new world after they elope from school also carry subtle tones of a romantic engagement between the two. In the final sequence of the film, *Sally's* response to *Nimmi* as she empathises with her despair and hopelessness is more aligned to the manner in which a male would treat his female partner in such a setting.

'*I will always be there for you. Have you still not understood my feelings for you?*' asks *Sally* of *Nimmi*.

In which case, the question of denial to gender identity must be raised. Was *Sally* an individual who represented a denial of gender role? Or was she also in denial of her gender identity? Did she seek in *Nimmi* a sexual companion? This remains for the viewer to interpret.

The film skilfully explores how gender roles are strongly linked to our emotional needs and may therefore shape our feelings of sexuality.

The climax of the film brings out *Sally's* ultimate commitment to *Nimmi* as they resort to suicide as the ultimate solution to their deep rooted conflicts.

Padmarajan's signature was the haunting climax of his films. In the climax of **Desatanakkilli Karayarilla,** *Sally and Nimmi find their safe niche.*

'Desatanakkilli Karayarilla,' true to the title, is the story of two socially alienated individuals who have never been rooted into society and therefore are analogous to migratory birds that have no homes, and that spend their lives migrating from place to place, to escape the unfavourable conditions that develop at a given place. The film reflects on how the insensitivity of society perpetuates their insecurity and alienation, culminating in a disastrous outcome.

The film expands the horizons of our minds and helps us overcome the taboos set by society. It teaches us to be more sensitive to individuals who manifest gender conflict by offering valuable insights into the factors that shape our perception of gender identity and gender role.

ATTENTION-SEEKING BEHAVIOUR IN MALAYALAM CINEMA

Mazhayethum Munpe[93] is one film that comes to the mind in the context of the exploration of attention-seeking behaviour in Malayalam Cinema. The plot of this film revolves around the pathological personality of **Shruthi**, characterized by persistent attention-seeking and self-centred behaviour.

The initial part of the film paints a character sketch of *Shruthi* through its narrative. *Shruthi* is portrayed as a college student who is lively, dramatic, vivacious, enthusiastic and flirtatious. She demonstrates a high need for attention in all her social circles. She gives undue importance to her external appearance and is always attentive to the tiniest details of her attire and cosmetic appeal. She makes a palpable effort to be the centre of attention at all times, oblivious to what the situation demands, going to great lengths and choosing inappropriate means to achieve this. She chooses to be loud, dramatic and eccentric in her mannerisms and statements in order to draw attention to herself. Her reaction to her new chemistry professor, *Nandakumar*, a young and handsome man with an impressive personality, is also centred on this unconscious drive. *Shruthi*'s loud and inappropriate entry into *Nandakumar*'s first lecture reflects her palpable need for attention.

***Annie** won the Filmfare Award for Best Actress- Malayalam, for her role in **Mazhayethum Munpe**. She plays the histrionic 'Shruthi' in this film.*

Shruthi is exaggerative in her display of emotions. She puts up an exaggerated display of innocence when her college principal demands an explanation for the cracker explosion in the classroom. She puts up a similar reaction when *Nandakumar* rushes to inquire into the cause of the frightening screams that are heard from her house. Also, *Shruthi* craves persistent stimulation. The insatiable need to break order, play pranks and throw unpleasant surprises at people, dominates her behaviour. She demonstrates an obvious lack of concern and sensitivity towards other people. Instead, she demonstrates egocentrism, self-indulgence, continuous longing for appreciation, and persistent manipulative behaviour in order to achieve her own needs.

Shruthi resists criticism. She reacts to criticism with hostility and vengeance. Though she demonstrates good social skills and draws a huge circle of friends, most of her social skills are manipulative and are directed at meeting her selfish needs. She demonstrates resistance towards seeing things realistically and refuses to acknowledge the gravity of situations and the emotions of other people.

The above cluster of symptoms skilfully sketches a ***histrionic personality***:

Histrionic personality disorder (HPD) *is defined by the American Psychiatric Association as a personality disorder characterized by a pattern of **excessive attention-seeking emotions**, usually beginning in early adulthood, including inappropriately seductive behaviour and an excessive need for approval. Histrionic people are lively, dramatic, vivacious, enthusiastic, and flirtatious. HPD affects four times as many **women** as men.*[29,30]

The classic features of this personality disorder include:

- *Provocative (or seductive) behaviour*
- *Relationships are considered more intimate than they actually are*
- *Attention-seeking*
- *Influenced easily by others or circumstances*
- *Speech (style) wants to impress; lacks detail*
- *Emotional lability; shallowness*
- *Make-up; physical appearance is used to draw attention to self*
- *Exaggerated emotions; theatrical*

Associated features include egocentrism, self-indulgence, continuous longing for appreciation, and persistent manipulative behaviour to achieve their own needs.[29,30]

Shruthi demonstrates a sense of superiority- a pride of her own personality and an unwillingness to change, viewing change as a threat. The pathological nature of this pride is evident in her reaction to the humiliation *Nandakumar* metes out to her in response to all her pranks. *Shruthi* begins to interpret this persistent criticism as a romantic interest on his part, and she expresses this thought to him. This thought-process is a reflection of the underlying confusion of her self-concept. She is unable to realistically process criticism, introspect and reflect on her behaviour, and embrace change. Instead, she demonstrates denial towards the negative aspects of her personality, and manipulates reality to confront criticism. The manipulation is an unconscious process, and not a deliberate one. She therefore truly believes that Nandakumar's constant criticism of her reflects his romantic interest in her.

Mammootty *as Nandakumar, Shruthi's chemistry professor and the object of her romantic interest*

Nandakumar is ignorant of the pathological nature of her behaviour and views it as a harmless infatuation that is bound to pass. He therefore takes her to visit his fiancé, *Uma*, who is in a state of paralysis and is undergoing *Ayurvedic* treatment for the same. Contrary to *Nandakumar's* expectations that revelation of this relationship will help *Shruthi* get over her infatuation, *Shruthi* reacts with hostility and vengeance to this fact. She becomes moody to an inappropriate degree as she realizes that the facts are not conducive to her self-fulfilment in this case. She refuses to accept this fact and remains in denial.

A turbulent *Shruthi* revisits *Uma* and manipulates reality to fulfil her selfish needs. *Shruthi* sets up a guilt trap, making *Uma* believe that *Nandakumar* only has a sympathetic interest in *Uma. Uma* is made to feel that she cannot fulfil *Nandakumar's* needs as a spouse, on account of her invalid state. Yet again, *Shruthi* is able to generate the conviction that is necessary for *Uma* to feel guilty.

Shobhana's *peak career as an actress in the Malayalam film industry was in the 80s and 90s. In **Mazhayethum Munpe**, she plays the invalid **Uma**, Nandakumar's fiancé .*

Following this visit, *Shruthi* goes home to her father, instead of going back to college. This represents her denial in confronting the ridicule of her peers. Until this point, the portrayal of behaviour and personality is in accordance with the features of *HPD*. Thereafter, the film goes on to depict a change in *Shruthi's* perspective as her father counsels her. *Shruthi* is shown as easily giving in. This aspect deviates from the true portrayal of *HPD*, for individuals with *HPD* are unable to view situations realistically, and refuse to come to terms with a loss. *Shruthi's* subsequent reactions of adaptation to the situation by being more realistic, expressing repentance and remorse at her act, do not fit into the *HPD* picture.

However, the climax of the film addresses the incidence of depression in individuals with *HPD*. As *Nandakumar* discovers the truth and abandons *Shruthi*, she goes into depression. She displays detachment and anhedonia, and eventually commits suicide.

*HPD may affect a person's social and/or romantic relationships, as well as their ability to cope with losses or failures. They may seek treatment for **clinical depression** when romantic (or other close personal) relationships end. Treatment is often prompted by depression associated with dissolved romantic relationships. Medication does little to affect the personality disorder, but may be helpful with symptoms such as depression.[31]*

The film also explores the background factors that have shaped *Shruthi's* personality. *Shruthi* is a child who has been raised by a single parent, for her mother apparently passed away in her childhood. Her father admits that his busy life did not permit adequate attention to her upbringing, and that she is therefore the outcome of both emotional deficiencies and excesses. While she missed out on a mother's love and a father's consistent presence, her father compensated for these deficiencies by providing her materialistic comforts and by refraining from criticism. The film portrays *Shruthi's* formative environment as one in which the child has missed out on many rewards in terms of parental appreciation, and at the same time, missed out on criticism.

*Psychoanalytic theories incriminate **authoritarian or distant attitudes** by one (mainly the mother) or both parents, along with **conditional love** based on expectations the child can never fully meet. Freud believed the lustfulness was a projection of the patient's lack of ability to love unconditionally and develop cognitively to maturity, and that such patients were overall emotionally shallow. He believed the reason for not being able to love could have been from a traumatic death experience of a close relative during childhood or divorce between parents, which gave a wrong impression of committed relationships.[30,32]*

*The exact cause of histrionic personality disorder is not known, but many mental health professionals believe that both learned and inherited factors play a role in its development. For example, the tendency for histrionic personality disorder to run in families suggests that a **genetic susceptibility** for the disorder might be inherited. However, the child of a parent with this disorder might simply be repeating **learned behaviour**. Other environmental factors that might be involved include a **lack of criticism** or punishment as a child, **conditional positive reinforcement** that is given only when a child completes certain approved behaviours, and **unpredictable attention** given to a child by his or her parent(s), all leading to confusion about what types of behaviour earn parental approval.[33]*

The film therefore makes an interesting case study of *Histrionic Personality Disorder*, in the light of the factors that contribute to such an entity.

EXPLORATION OF FRAGILE SELF-ESTEEM AND MENTAL ILLNESS IN MALAYALAM CINEMA

Vulnerability of the human spirit has been at the heart of the stories that have explored human behaviour in Malayalam cinema. Malayalam cinema has sensitively unveiled this vulnerability that lies at the core of a human being, beneath the layers of defence built in order to survive the assaults of an insensitive world on the psyche.

It is the path driven by this vulnerability that has been explored in a good many films.

Self-esteem is the way individuals think and feel about themselves and how well they do things that are important to them. In children, self-esteem is shaped by what they think and feel about themselves. Their self-esteem is highest when they see themselves as approximating their ideal self- the person they would like to be.[34]

Children with a high self-esteem have an easier time handling conflicts, resisting negative pressures, and making friends. They laugh and smile more and have a generally optimistic view of the world and their life.[35]

Children with low self-esteem have a difficult time dealing with problems, are overly self-critical, and can become passive, withdrawn, and depressed. They may hesitate to try new things, may speak negatively about themselves, are easily frustrated, and often see temporary problems as permanent conditions. They are pessimistic about themselves and their life.[35,36]

Oru Kadankatha Pole[94], *Ulsavapittennu*[95], *Manichithrathazhu*[96], *Sanmanassullavarkku Samadhanam*[97], *Ulladakkam*[98], *Sudinam*[99], *Ennu Swantham Janakikutty*[100], *Savidham*[101], *Neeyethra Dhanya*[102], *Chillu*[103], *Pranayavarnangal*[104], *Thooval Kottaram*[71]-the vulnerability and fragile self-esteem of the central character is the common factor in all these films, though the outcomes are different. Some of these films take us through the internal landscape of fragile characters that demonstrate *acceptance* of their negative circumstances, but eventually succumb to the chronic negativity and resort to suicide. Yet other films take us through the internal landscape of characters that demonstrate persistent *denial* and therefore resort to dissociation from reality or distortion of reality in order to cope with the harshness of their circumstances, taking the shape of psychosis of different forms.

Suicide as an outcome has been explored in a good many films.

The character of *Aniyan Thampuran* in **Ulsavapittennu**, *Vinodini* in **Sudinam**, *Sudha Thampuratty* in **Savidham**, *Shyama* in **Neeyethra Dhanya** and *Annie* in **Chillu**, represent characters whose fragile self-esteem and high need for positive regard culminates in suicide as the final outcome of the stressors in their lives. The behaviour of these characters is primarily governed by their need to subscribe to the social role that is expected of them and therefore win the positive regard of those around them. Their self-concept is significantly and pathologically rooted in this positive regard. They therefore put others ahead of themselves. In the process, they sacrifice their personal desires and dreams, becoming passive victims of their circumstances.

They see the ultimate meaning of their life in their relationships and fail to define the higher meaning of their lives.

Stressors that abolish this positive regard, create severe conflict and anxiety in them, for they represent individuals who derive their deepest motivation from such positive regard. It is in the setting of such conflict that these individuals resort to suicide.

> *The self desperately needs and seeks acceptance, love, warmth, care and reassurance from others. As a result, it is vulnerable. This need of the self is referred to as the need for **positive regard**. It is this need for positive regard that makes a person ignore inner signals and act in a way that pleases others, so as to get approval and support. So strong is this need that it may cause individuals to act contrary to what they feel is right, creating conflict.[37,38]*

Sudinam explores the character of *Vinodini* who takes on the role of a parent to her siblings, following the death of her parents. *Vinodini's* behaviour is driven by the need to fulfil this parental role and win the positive regard of her family and society. Contrary to the character of *Sharadammini* in **Chakoram**, *Vinodini* is in acceptance of her circumstances. There is thus none of the aggression in her behaviour that characterizes *Sharadammini's* personality.

Vinodini sacrifices her love for her sister's happiness, and comes to terms with this sacrifice. However, the misunderstanding and clashes in the family progressively increase, reducing the positive regard she has received from her family all along. Her sibling, *Appu*, is the only source of positive regard thereafter, and his untimely death thrusts her into deep anxiety as the only source of her positive regard is abolished. She gives in to the conflict created by the mounting stressors in her life and resorts to suicide.

Madhavi is best remembered for her portrayal of Unniyarcha in the National Award winning film, **Oru Vadakkan Veeragatha**. *She portrays the fragile* **'Vinodini' in Sudinam**.

Similarly, the plot of **Chillu** revolves around the vulnerable *Annie* who loses her mother early in her childhood. *Annie* seeks deep intimacy in all her relationships- a reflection of her intense need for positive regard. *Annie* derives the very meaning of her life from her relationships with people. However, *Annie* finds herself secluded as all her relationships abolish. As she loses all the sources of positive regard, she loses the meaning in her life. The conflict within her builds into deep anxiety, culminating in suicide. The film skilfully breathes life into '**Borderline Personality Disorder.**'

*Borderline personality disorder (**BPD**) is well known for its association with suicide; the suicide rate is 6–10% in this class of people.[39] People with BPD are highly sensitive to rejection and fear of possible abandonment. They display unusually intense sensitivity in their relationships, have difficulty regulating emotions and are impulsive. They feel emotions more easily and for longer than normal people. They are emotionally unstable due to repeated "re-firing" or re-initiation of an emotional reaction. They are exceptionally idealistic, joyful and loving. However, they are* *overwhelmed by negative emotions – they experience grief instead of sadness, humiliation instead of embarrassment, rage instead of anger and panic instead of nervousness.*[40,41,42]

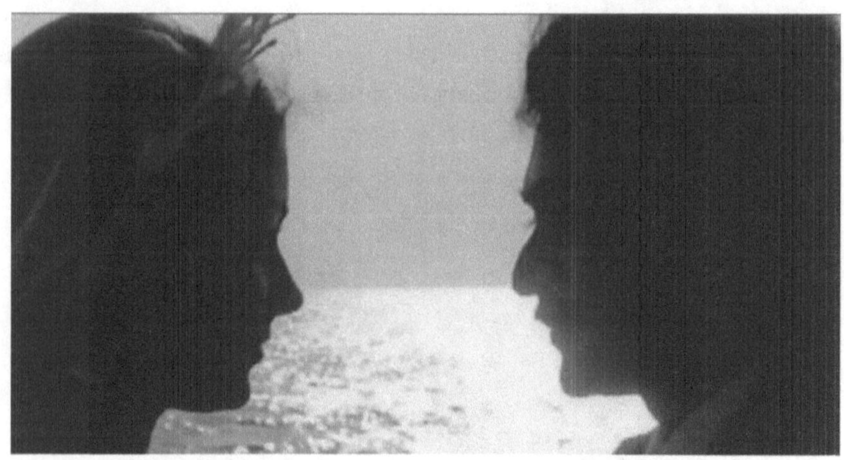

Shanthi Krishna and **Rony Vincent** *play the lead characters in Lenin Rajendran's* **Chillu:** *An exploration of 'Borderline Personality Disorder'*

Their suicidal behaviour reflects their efforts to escape from these intense negative emotions. They are aware of the intensity of their negative emotional reactions, but are unable to regulate them. They also depict emotional lability with mood swings.[43] *They express intense joy and gratitude at perceived expressions of kindness and intense sadness or anger at perceived criticism or hurtfulness. Their feelings towards others shift from positive to negative- from idealization to devaluation. They exhibit a strong desire for intimacy, but tend towards insecure, avoidant or fearfully preoccupied attachment patterns in relationships.*[41] *They often exhibit dissociation in response to a painful event, thus directing partial or full attention away from the painful event.*[42] *Most have a history of childhood trauma- particularly loss of caregivers in early childhood.*[44]

The character of *Aniyan Thampuran* in **Ulsavapittennu**, *Sudha Thampuratty* in **Savidham** and *Shyama* in **Neeyethra Dhanya,** explore a similar need for positive regard, and take us through different stressors that culminate in suicide.

The central character in all the above-mentioned films contrasts sharply with the self-actualized characters of Sudhakaran Nair in **Udyanapalakan** *or Ammini in* **Aranyakam** *who surpass their vulnerability by defining the higher meaning of their lives. Though these self-actualized characters guard* *a fragile self-esteem and therefore value and cherish relationships, they do not see the ultimate meaning of their life in relationships. Therefore, the failure of relationships does not cause them to lose motivation in life.*

The above-mentioned films have also shed light on the role of primary caregivers in the shaping of self-esteem. Most of the above characters are individuals who have lost a parent in their formative years.

Self-esteem comes from different sources for children at different stages of development. The development of self-esteem in young children is heavily influenced by parental attitudes and behaviour. Supportive parental behaviour, including encouragement and praise for accomplishments, as well as the child's internalization of the parents' own attitudes toward success and failure, are the most powerful factors in the development of self-esteem in early childhood.

When parental involvement is limited, children typically receive scant mirroring or encouragement. They have no one reflecting back to them that they are worthwhile, admirable, or interesting. Thus, the development of self-confidence and self-esteem are compromised.[45,46]

Oru Kadankatha Pole, Sanmanassullavarkku Samadhanam, Ulladakkam and **Pranayavarnangal** are films that have explored vulnerable personalities who demonstrate denial to stressors, contrary to the characters discussed above that demonstrate acceptance. These films illustrate how neurotic and psychotic behaviour is rooted in the phenomenon of denial.

These films explore the impact of an acute stressor on such a personality.

The character of *Mr. Warrier* in **Oru Kadankatha Pole**, is that of an introvert who is vulnerable, compassionate and gentle in his ways. He restricts himself to a closed and confined world, largely leading a solitary life, with few close companions. He attributes immense significance to living up to the role of a 'gentleman' in his relationships, prioritizing the emotions and needs of others over his own needs, reflecting his immense need for positive regard.

'Am I loveable and likeable?' is strongly seeded into his behaviour and his personality reflects his uncertainty with regard to this question. His introversion represents an underlying fear of rejection, reflecting his fragile self-esteem. He therefore fails at being assertive in his relationships. This interferes with his ability to express himself freely in a relationship. He fails to express his true feelings to *Radha*, the lady whom he loves. His fear of rejection manifests as

confusion with regard to expressing his emotions, and this eventually creates a misunderstanding in his relationship. His friends also misunderstand him and refuse to give him an opportunity to explain and clarify. This misunderstanding destroys all the sources of positive regard in his life. He is unable to come to acceptance of this misunderstanding and his failure at clearing it. The deep conflict and denial that result on account of the trauma caused to a fragile self-esteem precipitate an acute anxiety state, causing him to seek medical help.

Nedumudi Venu plays the role of the fragile 'Mr Warrier' in **Oru Kadankatha Pole**

The character of *Arathi* in **Pranayavarnangal** is similar in terms of the introversion and vulnerability. *Arathi* lives in a solitary world of her own- a world of books and poems, with a limited circle of friends. She is fragile and demonstrates irrational fears. This is illustrated in her inability to overcome her deep rooted fear of the *Kaliyattam* demigod processions that are part of the tradition and culture of her native village. The childhood stories that she has heard of these demigods continue to terrify her, representing unresolved conflict in her mind. Her cognitive resources fail to rationalize and resolve this conflict and overcome her fear. She therefore demonstrates a tendency towards denial.

It is perhaps her introversion that attracts her to *Maya*'s extroverted personality, and the two become thick friends. *Maya* plays a prank on *Arathi* and leads her to believe that *Vinayachandran*, the writer she admires, has a romantic interest in her. *Arathi* derives motivation from the positive regard his words feed her with, and grows extremely dependent on his touch to her life. When *Arathi* encounters the truth and witnesses *Vinayachandran's* marriage with *Maya*, her mind refuses to come to terms with this truth. This denial manifests as acute anxiety and a transient psychotic episode in the form of dissociation.

Manju Warrier is recognized as one of the finest actresses in Malayalam Cinema. She established her potential as an actress by her breathtaking performance in the film **Sallapam**. *She plays the fragile and introverted 'Arathi' in* **Pranayavarnangal**.

Sanmanassullavarkku Samadhanam narrates the story of *Meera*, a young girl who accidentally becomes the cause of her father's death from electrocution. *Meera's* father is the breadwinner of the family and runs the household, shouldering all the responsibilities of the family. A fragile and vulnerable *Meera* is unable to come to acceptance of the loss of the responsible male figure in her life and her vulnerable mind displays denial towards this tragedy. That she is responsible for this tragedy makes her denial profound. This manifests as acute anxiety and dissociation. *Meera* is admitted for psychotherapy, but she recovers completely in due course of time and comes to terms with the loss. She takes on the role of breadwinner, and goes about her life with no residues of the psychosis.

Karthika** as the fragile 'Meera' in **Sanmanassullavarkku Samadhanam

Ulladakkam narrates the story of *Reshma*, a young girl who loses her mother in childhood and is raised by her sibling. *Reshma*'s first episode of psychosis is in response to her mother's death, when she reacts violently to the trauma on account of her denial to it. *Reshma*'s psychotic episode is characterized by **dissociation**, a neurotic defense mechanism wherein there is temporary drastic modification of one's personal identity or character to avoid emotional distress. The aggression and violent behaviour shields her young and vulnerable mind from the severity of the emotions generated by the trauma.

However, *Reshma* gradually recovers from this acute episode and grows up to be an individual with a rich inner world. She is portrayed as a cheerful and zealous individual with varied interests, including books, music and dance. The film skilfully explores how deep vulnerability can lay concealed beneath the defenses one builds.

Reshma writes numerous letters to her deceased mother in her diaries. Her diary brings to light her rich imagination. She fantasizes her mother as a star in the sky, and holds silent conversations with the night sky. She fantasizes rain as the love and affection that her mother sends across from the distant world of the stars. Through her rich fantasy, she lives her unfulfilled longing for a mother's love and affection. She therefore uses ***fantasy*** as a defense mechanism to cope with her mother's absence. This immature defense mechanism of fantasy reflects her denial to her mother's absence.

Reshma's second episode of psychosis is in response to the death of her boyfriend, *Arun*. The psychosis clearly takes the form of ***dissociation***, wherein *Reshma* dissociates from her internal feelings of intense pain and sorrow and avoids feeling them by switching to violent aggression. The film sensitively explores the plot of ***post-traumatic stress disorder (PTSD)***.

Reshma is portrayed as an individual who has never really come to terms with the loss of her mother. She remains in denial, the event of her mother's death largely alienated by her fragile mind through dissociation and repression, persisting in her unconscious as an unresolved conflict.

*Most individuals react with shock and disbelief when faced with a harrowing ordeal (realistic anxiety). In the weeks and months to follow, they may also experience nightmares, episodes of intrusive thoughts and images, as well as hyper arousal. In time, however, they are able to process and incorporate such negative events into their views of the world and self and are able to carry on with their lives. On the other hand, some individuals, especially children, have difficulty coping with traumatic experiences and integrating such events into their psyche. These experiences may be **repressed** and **dissociated** from consciousness, only to re-emerge later in the context of disorders such as **Post Traumatic Stress Disorder**.*[47]

Arun's death mimics the trauma of her childhood, and awakens in her the memories of a repressed event, reactivating the unresolved conflict.

*In Freud's view, not only does repressed trauma re-emerge later in life, it also reactivates previously repressed but unresolved conflicts from childhood. The combined anxiety (**neurotic anxiety**) resulting from the reawakening of this earlier conflict and from the more recent trauma results in other defense mechanisms such as **regression, denial, reaction formation and undoing**, which are all responsible for some of the symptoms of **PTSD**.* [48]

Amala Akkineni *is remembered in the Malayalam film industry for her role in* **Ulladakkam** *and* **Ente Sooryaputhrikku**. *She plays the character of the fragile* **'Reshma'** *in* **Ulladakkam**, *for which she received the Filmfare Award for Best Actress-Malayalam.*

Reshma's psychosis is characterized by *depersonalization, derealisation and anhedonia-* the classic features of *PTSD*. She demonstrates detachment, failing to respond to her own needs and to her surroundings. Instead, she perceives the approach of her family members and others towards her as a potential threat. Even as the aggression and violence subside with medication, she remains detached, with a palpable lack of interest in her environment.

> *Regression to an early stage of development, such as the oral stage which was characterized by ego disorganization, could result in some of the numbing symptoms characteristic of PTSD. These include* **depersonalization** *(feeling detached from one's mental processes or body),* **derealization** *(experiencing the external world as strange or unreal) and* **anhedonia** *(an inability to experience pleasure from normally pleasurable activities).*[49]

Reshma reveals in the course of her psychiatric consultation that she often dreams of her mother, but she does not report any nightmares. However, individuals with *PTSD* often report nightmares that are reflections of their repressed traumatic memories and unresolved conflicts.

> *According to Freud, the need for repressed material to enter consciousness is more powerful than the pleasure principle. So despite the best efforts of the individual to keep memories of the experience repressed, the psyche forces them into consciousness. The purpose is that by reliving the experience, the ego thereby tries to master and reduce the anxiety. At first, the events are repeated in dreams and nightmares over which there is no conscious control, and later on in waking hours.*[50]

The major symptom of *PTSD* is the re-experiencing of trauma wherein the individual repeats the repressed memory as a contemporary experience instead of remembering it as something in the past. This is clearly evident in *Reshma*'s case, wherein numerous associations continue to trigger episodes of dissociation on account of re-surfacing of the repressed trauma. Her phobia of the sea, her turbulence at the sight of the percussionists in the band, the **transference** she demonstrates towards *Dr Sunny*, are all reflections of the unconscious associations her mind forms between objects/people and the trauma of *Arun*'s death. *Reshma* continues to repress the trauma of *Arun*'s death and these emotions resurface when she is exposed to these associations. In the climax of the film, the percussionists in the band trigger the repressed memory of *Arun*'s death, and *Reshma*'s mind regresses to the past- to the unresolved conflict of *Arun*'s death, which is in reality, an event of the past.

The film is therefore brilliant in its psychological perspective of *PTSD*, for it explores the background factors, especially childhood experiences, personality, psychological basis and the manifestations of *PTSD*. The film successfully translates the complex science of *PTSD* into an insightful story for the common man, shaping society's attitude to such disorders.

Pavithram[105] is yet another film whose climax culminates in *PTSD*. The central character of this film, *Unnikrishnan*, abandons his dreams and personal goals in life and commits to the role of a parent to his baby sister, *Meenakshi*. Thereafter, he invests the entire meaning of his life in this role. However, his sister fails to see this act of sacrifice and chooses a path of her own, progressively detaching herself from his life. *Unnikrishnan* fears losing her and is in denial of this outcome. This denial manifests as the fierce possessiveness he demonstrates towards *Meenakshi*, and the strong control he exercises on her life. As *Meenakshi* distances and the loneliness in his life increases, he makes a last attempt at self-preservation by approaching *Meera*, the woman whose love he had sacrificed in order to take on the role of a parent to his sister. But *Meera's* circumstances prevent her from accepting his proposal, and *Unnikrishnan* is compelled to confront his fears, towards which he continues to maintain denial. The denial takes on a serious note when he witnesses *Meenakshi* meet with an accident, and the acute anxiety culminates in dissociation. Though the symptoms that *Unnikrishnan* demonstrates in the climax, especially in terms of depersonalization and derealisation are typical of *PTSD*, what is perhaps lacking in the film is a background for *PTSD*. Unlike *Reshma's* character in **Ulladakkam**, this film does not offer childhood trauma and the consequent moulding of a personality as a background for *PTSD*. There is the palpable lack of repression in the background.

Pavithram was recognized for its plot that portrayed a unique scenario of conflict. Mohanlal plays the lead character 'Unnikrishnan' in this film- a role that fetched him the Filmfare Award for Best Actor in 1994.

Since not all persons who experience trauma actually develop PTSD, what differentiates those who do from those who do not? A traumatic event leads to the development of PTSD if the victim has a pre-existing psychological structure that can be understood as Freud's actual neurosis. This pre-existing structure prevents the individual from processing the traumatic incident in a normal, symbolic or representational way, which is the main problem in PTSD.[51]

This chapter would be incomplete without a mention of the film ***Innale*** that explores a case of ***dissociative amnesia,*** a condition that represents a greater degree of dissociation and repression. Directed by *P.Padmarajan*, the plot of ***Innale*** revolves around a young orphan girl, *Maya*, who meets with a major accident, and awakens from her comatose state to discover that she has no memory of her past.

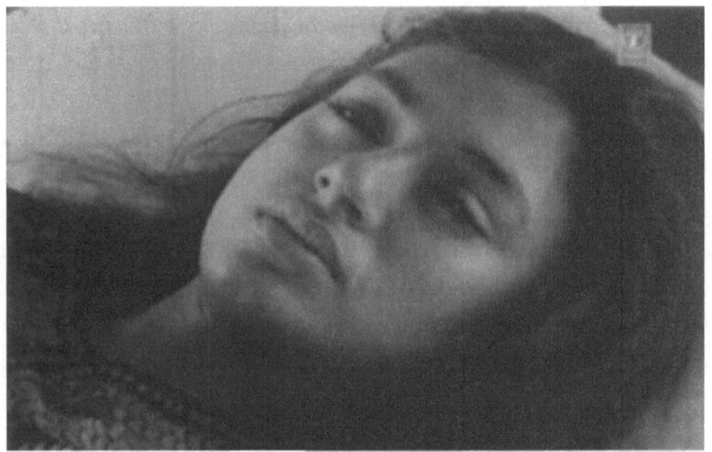

Innale *was a film that questioned the very foundation on which the reality of human life is erected.* **Shobhana** *played the character of the amnesic* **'Maya'** *in this film-a role that fetched her the Filmfare Award for Best Actress in 1990*

Padmarajan's portrayal of dissociative amnesia is in close alignment to the clinical presentation of this condition. Dissociative amnesia can occur without any structural damage to the brain, as is the case in this film. *Maya*'s brain scans and other tests are reported as normal. Dissociative amnesia often occurs due to a traumatic situation that individuals wish to consciously or unconsciously avoid. *Maya* draws similarity with *Reshma* in that she guards a fragile mind beneath her apparent autonomy and zeal. Analogous to *Reshma*'s reaction,

Maya's mind rejects the reality of the accident in order to overcome the intense anxiety, activating severe dissociation and repression.

> **Dissociative amnesia** *is defined as one or more episodes of inability to recall important personal information, usually of a traumatic or stressful nature, that is too extensive to be explained by ordinary forgetfulness.*[52]

> *The common presentation for Dissociative amnesia is amnesia for personal identity and traumatic details, but intact memory for general information. The amnesia is usually only anterograde, restricted to the period following the trauma, and is without problems with regard to learning new information. Individuals with dissociative amnesia are cognitively intact and function coherently.*[53]

> *Dissociation is conceptualized as a basic part of the psychobiology of the human trauma response– a protective activation of altered states of consciousness in response to overwhelming psychological trauma. Memories relating to the trauma are encoded during these altered states. When the person returns to the baseline state, there is relatively less access to the dissociated information, leading to amnesia for at least some part of the traumatic event. Not only is there amnesia for the trauma, but the person frequently has dissociated the fact that certain basic assumptions of the self, relationships, other people and the nature of the world, have been altered by the trauma. However, the dissociated memories can manifest themselves as posttraumatic nightmares, re-enactments, intrusive imagery and somatoform symptoms.*[54]

"*The most beautiful people we have known are those who have known defeat, known suffering, known struggle, known loss, and have found their way out of the depths. These persons have an appreciation, a sensitivity, and an understanding of life that fills them with compassion, gentleness, and a deep loving concern. Beautiful people do not just happen.***"**

- Elisabeth Kubler-Ross

Dissociation And Fantasy In Malayalam Cinema

Ennu Swantham Janakikutty[100] and *Manichithrathazhu*[96] were films that were revolutionary for they broke out of the conventional themes of mental illness portrayed in cinema and went on to explore the complexity of **dissociative disorders**. These were perhaps the few films that not only shed light on the factors that shaped dissociative disorders, but also succeeded in giving these disorders a human touch. The sensitivity with which the central character of these films is explored, dissolves the barriers we create in our minds with regard to mental illness. Both these films explore a category of dissociative disorders referred to as '**Dissociative identity disorder**.'

> **Dissociative disorders** *are conditions that involve disruptions or breakdown of memory, awareness, identity, or perception.*[55]

> **Dissociative identity disorder** *(formerly multiple personality disorder) refers to a condition characterized by the alternation of two or more distinct personality states with impaired recall among personality states. In extreme cases, the host personality is unaware of the other, alternating personalities. However, the alternate personalities are aware of all the existing personalities.*[55,56]

As discussed in the previous chapter, the central character of both these films is an individual with a fragile self-esteem.

Janakikutty in **Ennu Swantham Janakikutty** is an adolescent girl who grows up in an environment with emotional neglect. Her relationship with her father is distant for he is away on work, and is unable to demonstrate significant attachment to his family. Her mother represents a conventional stereotype who is always preoccupied with the household chores and with her own emotional conflicts, paying little attention to the emotional needs of her daughter. *Janakikutty*'s cousins do not provide her with close companionship; they alienate her from their emotional world. Her brother also demonstrates neglect towards her need for companionship. *Janakikutty* is therefore thrust into a solitary world of her own. This perhaps explains her fragile self-esteem;

neglect and alienation seed in her a sense of worthlessness. '*Am I likeable and worthy of love and appreciation?*' remains an unanswered question in her mind.

*In 1997, **Jomol** won the Kerala State Film Award for best actress for her role in **Ennu Swantham Janakikutty** and also a special jury mention from the National Film Awards.*

Ganga in **Manichithrathazhu** is also an outcome of childhood neglect. *Ganga*'s childhood is spent in the care and attention of her grandmother as her parents are preoccupied with their jobs and are emotionally unavailable to *Ganga*. The film does not shed light on the nature of the attachment between *Ganga* and her grandmother. In any case, the emotional neglect contributes to a fragile self-esteem that lies at the heart of her personality.

*The films subsequently explore the disposition of these characters towards **fantasy**.*

Janakikutty is an ardent daydreamer and listens with avidity to the tales narrated by the *Muthassi* (grandmother) who comes to visit the family. *Janakikutty* demonstrates such extensive and deep involvement in fantasy that she does not question the truth in the stories narrated by the old lady. The source of this disposition to fantasy is perhaps a parent, grandparent, teacher, or friend who filled her world with fairy tales when she was a child, overexposing her young mind to fantasy. *Janakikutty* therefore demonstrates immense potential for imagination and the fantasy comes in as a source of pleasure to her young mind.

Her mind learns to use fantasy as a source of escape from the unpleasant emotions that trouble her fragile mind. As a child, the line between fantasy and reality in her mind is thin. Fantasy allows her to experience emotions as vivid as real world experiences. The child therefore unconsciously substitutes real world stimuli with fantasy in the setting of trauma, to escape from the unpleasant feelings. Fantasy becomes her predominant unconscious defense mechanism in the setting of trauma.

Ganga shares similarities with *Janakikutty* with regard to fantasy as an important ingredient of her childhood. Her childhood is dominated by the fantasy stories, folklores and myths that are narrated by her grandmother, and by the ritualistic behaviour adopted by her grandmother. *Ganga's* personality parallels *Janakikutty's* personality in adopting fantasy as a defense mechanism to escape the unpleasant feelings created by the stressors in her life.

An important cause for overindulgence with fantasy is parents or carers who provide a very structured and imaginative mental or play environment during childhood. People with fantasy prone personalities are more likely to have had parents, or close family members that made their inanimate toys as children seem real. They also encourage the child to believe in imaginary companions, read fairytales all through childhood and re-enact the things they have read. People who were involved in creative fantasy activities like piano, ballet and drawing at a young age are more likely to obtain a fantasy prone personality. Acting is also a way for children to identify as different people and characters which can make the child prone to fantasy-like dreams as they grow up. This can cause the person to grow up thinking they have experienced certain things and they can visualize a certain occurrence from the training they obtained while being involved in plays.[57,58]

People have reported that they believed their dolls and stuffed animals were living creatures and that their parents encouraged them to indulge in their fantasies and daydreams.[59]

These films draw important psychological conclusions. They shed light on the interaction between a fragile self-esteem and trauma in childhood, when cognition is not fully developed. They highlight how a child with a fragile self-esteem demonstrates a tendency to avoid the internalization of trauma at an unconscious level (denial), demonstrating ***dissociation***. They also highlight how the child switches to fantasy in the dissociated state in order to distort reality and come to terms with the trauma. As the child grows, he or she becomes conditioned to dissociate and switch to fantasy, for it succeeds in relieving the unpleasant feelings. However, the dissociation and failure to internalize traumatic experiences, affects the normal development of cognition. This lack of cognition can in turn lead to progressive distortion of reality as the child grows, breeding the ground for full-fledged psychiatric disorders in the future.

An important comparison in this context is the character of *Ammini* in *Aranyakam*. Why is it that *Ammini*, despite a fragile self-esteem and a rich imaginative world and exposure to fantasy, grows up to be a self-actualized individual? The answer lies in her acceptance of trauma and its internalization. *Ammini* comes to terms with the equation of her life early in her childhood, and is comfortable with the experience of unpleasant feelings. This acceptance prevents her from a need to dissociate from unpleasant feelings. Therefore, her mind does not activate the pathological defense mechanisms that characterize the personalities of *Janakikutty* and *Ganga*. *Ammini's* cognition and ego demonstrate a high intentionality and she is able to find within herself conditions of worth that overcome her fragile self-esteem.

> *Several studies have reported that dissociation and fantasy proneness are highly correlated. This suggests the possibility that the dissociated selves are a coping response to trauma. However, a lengthy review of the evidence concludes that there is strong empirical support for the hypothesis that dissociation is caused primarily and directly by exposure to trauma, and that fantasy is of secondary importance.* [60]

Janakikutty's first episode of psychosis is in response to the awareness of the relationship between her romantic interest, *Bhaskaran*, and her cousin *Sarojini*. *Bhaskaran* represents an important influence in *Janakikutty's* life for she views him as the only source of positive reinforcement. *Bhaskaran* takes an interest in *Janakikutty*, bringing her little gifts and engaging in conversations that make her feel worthy. His presence in her life comes as a reassuring answer to the question she has struggled with all along: *'Am I worthy of being liked and loved?'* His interest in her becomes an important source of her motivation at this point in her life. She gives it a romantic dimension in her mind. When she is exposed to the nature of the relationship between *Bhaskaran* and *Sarojini*, she is unable to come to terms with it. To her fragile mind, their relationship confirms her feelings of worthlessness and she demonstrates denial to these unpleasant feelings. This reflects her inability to find within herself conditions of worth and her resultant dependence on external sources of positive reinforcement to nurture her self-esteem. The denial and deep anxiety thus created trigger dissociation and adoption of fantasy as defense mechanisms.

Distortion results when an individual tries to live predominantly to the conditions of worth (discussed previously in Chapter 5) and develops a discrepancy between what the person feels is right and how the person actually acts. In order to deal with the incongruence, the individual must deny his or her true feelings or distort them. Non-availability of ideas or experiences pertaining to their self-concept facilitates such distortion. Individuals with excessively rigid and strict conditions of worth or narrowly defined self-concepts are particularly prone to deny and distort their experiences.[17,18]

*Ganga (**Shobhana**) demonstrates a pathological affinity to the legendary character Nagavalli, a Bharathanatyam dancer who is believed to have been killed by a cruel ancestor by name Shankaran Thampi. Ganga is fascinated by stories of Nagavalli's bloodthirsty spirit haunting the ancestral house.*

Ganga's first episode of psychosis is in response to the stress precipitated by examinations when she is in high school. This might reflect the overt significance she attributes to performance in examinations as a positive reinforcement to her fragile self-esteem. The anxiety of performing triggers her first episode of psychosis. She demonstrates agitation and dissociation, and is eventually taken to a psychiatrist by her parents. The episode abates and *Ganga* goes on to lead a normal life. However, there is the palpable lack of a stressor in *Ganga's* second episode of psychosis when she moves to the '*Madampalli Tharavadu*' with *Nakulan*, her husband. *Ganga's* marriage is portrayed as a turbulence-free relationship and *Nakulan* is depicted as a sensible and sensitive husband, responsive to *Ganga's* emotional needs. In the absence of marital discord and other stressors, *Ganga* resorts to dissociation and fantasy. This portrayal lacks a scientific basis for it does not demonstrate the need for adoption of an unconscious defense mechanism. Here, the plot of the film loses its conviction.

When *Janakikutty* switches her identity to fantasy, her new identity continues to retain awareness of her fundamental identity. She recognizes her family members and is fairly oriented to the details of her environment. Her fantasy adds additional elements to her perception and she is unable to differentiate these from reality. However, *Ganga* in her dissociated state loses awareness of her fundamental identity and fails to recognize her family members. She loses orientation to time, place and person. Her alter-ego represents an identity with a distinct autobiographical memory of its own.

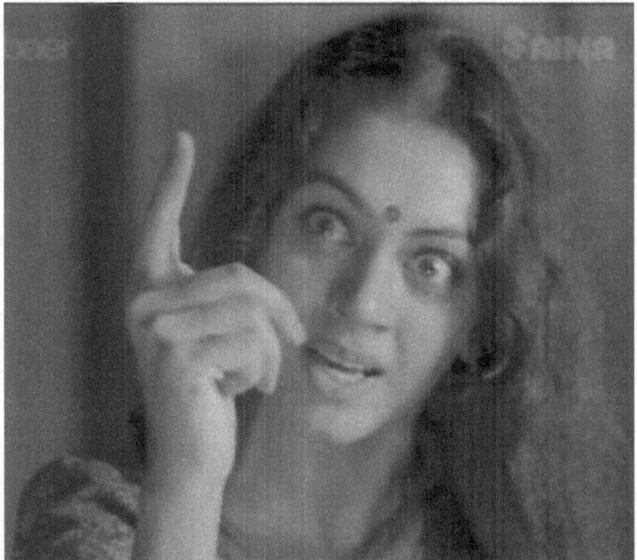

Shobhana demonstrates her versatility by effortlessly switching between the passive 'Ganga' and the aggressive alter-ego 'Nagavalli.' She won the National Film Award for Best Actress for her performance in the film.

The identities in Dissociative Identity Disorder may be unaware of each other and compartmentalize knowledge and memories, resulting in chaotic personal lives.[61]

> *The primary identity, which often has the patient's given name, tends to be passive, dependent, guilty and depressed while the alter-ego tends to be more active, aggressive or hostile, often containing a current time line that lacks childhood memory. Most identities are of ordinary people, though fictional, mythical, celebrity and animal parts have been reported.*[62]

The alter-ego of both *Janakikutty* and *Ganga*, demonstrate behaviour that contradicts their fundamental traits of passivism and helplessness.

The two films adopt different routes to a resolved climax. *Janakikutty* is eventually hospitalized, but the conflict pertaining to *Bhaskaran* abates as *Sarojini* abandons *Bhaskaran* and moves on with her life and gets married in accordance with her family's wishes. The climax of the film portrays a relaxed and cured *Janakikutty*, bidding goodbye to her fantasy character as her mind finds comfort and reassurance in the renewed care and attention from *Bhaskaran*.

On the contrary, *Ganga*'s condition worsens despite the absence of a stressor and the psychiatrist anticipates a permanent transformation of her fundamental personality to the alter-ego. This assumption with regard to her prognosis lacks a scientific basis. The subsequent plot of the film and the climax is largely fictional.

> *Little is known about the prognosis of untreated Dissociative Identity Disorder. It rarely, if ever, goes away without treatment, but symptoms may resolve from time to time or wax and wane spontaneously. Suicidal ideation, failed suicide attempts, and self-harm also occur. Duration of treatment can vary depending on patient goals, which can extend from elimination of all alters to merely reducing inter-alter amnesia, but generally takes years.*[61,63,64]

"And those who were seen dancing were thought to be insane by those who could not hear the music."

- Friedrich Nietzsche

CONCLUSION

The films mentioned under different themes in this book are valuable in the inferences they draw with regard to the factors that shape mental health. They breathe life into the ***theories of personality*** and also provide valuable insights with regard to the roots of mental illness, particularly dissociative disorders.

Vulnerability is at the heart of all these films. The films explore the diverse paths adopted by this vulnerability, culminating in variable outcomes that include self-actualization, deviant behaviour (aggression), personality disorders, dissociative disorders and suicide. They skilfully demonstrate the dynamic interaction between the vulnerable self and environmental stressors in the nurturing of personality. They explore the factors that steer this vulnerability towards creativity and self-actualization on one hand and towards mental unrest on the other hand. They address an important research question- Are creativity and mental illness two sides of the same coin?

These films emphasize the ***role of parenting*** in the healthy nurturing of self-esteem and personality. They explore reactions to stress and educate the common man on the nature of the psychological defense mechanisms that are activated in response to stress. They make a distinction between healthy and pathological defense mechanisms. They illustrate how healthy defense mechanisms pave the path to self-actualization. They emphasize the role of acceptance and cognition in the adoption of healthy defense mechanisms. They explore pathological defense mechanisms and demonstrate how these are rooted in denial. These films establish the link between denial, pathological defense mechanisms and mental illness.

All in all, they sensitize us to how human the phenomenon of mental illness is. They help us embrace the eccentricities, oddities and insanities that characterize human life and therefore erase the stigma associated with mental illness.

"*I became insane with long intervals of horrible sanity.*"
- Edgar Allan Poe

These films are nothing short of psychology textbooks for they translate the complex theories of personality and mental integrity into palatable and motivating stories that can be comprehended by the common man. They are therefore of spiritual importance and shape our attitude to mental health. They guide us with respect to discovering within ourselves the answers to the complexities in our lives.

Perhaps it is in this context that films such as **_Thanmathra_**[107] and **_Vadakkumnathan_**[108] failed, despite the significance of the mental health themes that they focussed on. **_Thanmathra_** centred its theme on _Alzheimer's disease_ while **_Vadakkumnathan_** attempted a sketch of _bipolar disorder_. What is common to both films is that the story feeds off the label. The story reduces the abstract infinity of the human mind to the confines of a label as opposed to the films discussed earlier in this book that delve into the abstract of the human mind and blur labels. These films therefore lack in psychological essence for they are devoid of the core component that defines good cinema. These films are defined by their label, and not by their narrative. It is important to understand that there is more insight and realism in stories borrowed from the study of life than in stories created from the study of labels and diagnoses.

> _An artist must demonstrate a deep curiosity to study the ground realities of life and bring out the essence thus discovered into the medium of a story. True art is always a quest, and one must demonstrate a genuine commitment to this quest._

There are also films that have merely used mental illness as an ingredient of the plot, rather than as the central theme. **_Thalavattam_**[109], **_Mookilla Rajyathu_**[110] and **_Kilukkam_**[111] are a few films in this regard. While it is clear that the objective of these films is not centred on mental illness and that mental illness is brought in to provide humour and entertainment, one wonders if this is ethical.

Mohanlal _and_ **_Sukumari_** _in the film_ **_Thalavattam_**_, loosely adapted from Ken Kesey's novel 'One flew over the Cuckoo's nest'_

While fiction is an artist's freedom, one wonders if fiction in the context of mental illness is ethical. Considering that films play a significant role in shaping the common man's perception of human conditions, there is perhaps a need to question this freedom from an ethical point of view.

I conclude this book in the belief that it will serve as a guide with regard to introspection and reflection on the psychological value of current cinema. There is an urgent need for film makers to introspect on the purpose that cinema must serve, over and above entertainment. Similarly, there is a need to shape public attitude towards what qualifies for good cinema and educate people with regard to the significance of good cinema in the context of the psychological need it subserves.

"The stories are all around us. It is for us to find them and empower them with our story-telling ability."

PART II

A NARRATIVE OF THE FILMS

ARANYAKAM

Aranyakam (*The forests*)…

Man's deepest instincts feed off the forests to which he belongs.

"The forests and I was all there was. In the deep still silence, I could feel the earth's beating heart.**"**

Directed by **Hariharan,** and written by **M.T.Vasudevan Nair,** *Aranyakam*[66] is an insightful study of personality. It probes into the evolution of personality in the light of circumstantial factors, and offers deep insights into human behaviour.

The personality of **Ammini** is at the heart of this film. The film primarily dwells on the resilience that a vulnerable *Ammini* demonstrates in the setting of the tragedies in her life. *Ammini*'s personality forms an inspirational reference for the creative potential of a vulnerable mind.

The film unfolds with an older *Ammini*, returning after decades to the forests that guard her most cherished memories- forests that embody perceptions from a phase of her life that she holds closest to her heart.

I return...
Oh beautiful moments I have lost,
With flowers in my heart
I return today
to seek your graves...
I have often cried in your reminiscence...
I have also laughed in your reminiscence...
Where are those jungles on which my childhood fantasies once grazed, in the quest for the beautiful words that would give them meaning?
Where are those jungle trails on which beads once scattered from the garlands of fantasy clouds, only to disintegrate?

This poetic, lyrical note on which the film unfolds, introduces us to the rich, imaginative world that thrives in *Ammini's* mind. Perhaps she is a writer or a journalist.

Saleema plays the imaginative and fantasy-prone 'Ammini' in Aranyakam

The film then transports us to her past- to the forests that form the backdrop of her memories, the forests that were instrumental in her perceptions and fantasies.

The film introduces an adolescent *Ammini* who is just back home from boarding school. It introduces us to the other members of her family- her

Valiyachan (uncle), *Valiyamma* (aunt), her cousins *Shylaja* and *Anu*, and her grandfather who is now slowly fading away.

Ammini is an orphan whose mother passed away when she was a child, and whose father remarried and moved on to a new life in *Delhi*. *Ammini* grows up with her *Valiyachan*'s family, spending a significant part of her life in boarding school.

'*St. Joseph's Girls' Prison,*' she mocks.

Her only connection with her father is the money he sends on occasion, the gifts he occasionally buys her, and the rare occasions when father and daughter meet. She cherishes these little tokens and refuses to ask for more. She chooses to build her life on her own, accepting the reality of her life, rather than be devastated by her father's rejection. She transforms her life of solitude into a world of fantasy.

The forest is *Ammini*'s home. The rich wilderness of the forest shields her from the harshness of her circumstances and from the insensitivity of fellow human beings. She takes to the companionship of the trees, birds and streams that throb with life and feed her spirit with imagination. The forests teach her to see the richness and possibility in life. The film skilfully portrays her deep relationship with nature.

This relationship is explored in the song:

> **'*Olichirikkan vallikudilonnu orukki vachille,*
> *Kallichirikkan kathaparayan killimakal vannile.*'**
> *(Haven't the creepers carved a hideout for you?*
> *Hasn't the little bird come to play and narrate stories?)*

Ammini is portrayed as imaginative and adventurous. The film then explores her deep sensitivity and vulnerability. *Ammini* masks her vulnerability with her eccentricity. In a solitary world where she has never had the luxury of the kind of companionship where she can share her joys and unburden her sorrows, *Ammini* learns to keep her emotions to herself. She lives her life with gay abandon- an approach detested by her cousins and other family members, who hold on to traditional roles. She cleverly masks the feminine spirit that throbs within her, refusing to acknowledge its emotional needs.

The film dwells on the essence of womanhood:

Delicate, fragile, exquisitely beautiful. Incapable of sustenance in adversity. Its need for the most sensitive, tender, loving care.

Ammini harbours within her a feminine spirit that is unable to articulate in the real world for it is vulnerable and fears rejection.

The film therefore demonstrates how rejection by primary caregivers can influence the evolution of a personality by its impact on self-esteem, seeding an unconscious fear of rejection.

Ammini pretends to be rather unfeminine. She is loud and crude, forever mocking the stereotyped ways of the world. She laughs away the issues that are regarded as significant by her cousins, and instead, dwells upon issues that are of no significance to them. While her cousins live up to the traditional feminine roles defined by contemporary society, *Ammini* earns the label of eccentricity and madness. Her cousins fail to realize that this eccentricity and madness are in reality, coping mechanisms that mask her deep vulnerability.

Ammini chooses to celebrate her solitude. She roams the forests and her expeditions lead her to the discovery of places that provide her the luxury of solitary engagement with her perceptions for these places are little known to others. An old temple ruin, concealed by overgrown climbers and creepers, is her nook. Here, she sits down to scribble random thoughts into a notebook- her notebook of madness, as she calls it. But in truth, it is the sorrow of her wounded spirit that she liberates in these mad ramblings. She writes letters to celebrities- writers and leaders. Letters that she never posts.

In her ability to laugh at herself, one almost fails to see the vulnerability she conceals within.

The film then goes on to explore relationships in the context of personality.

In the course of her wanderings in the forest, *Ammini* runs into a stranger who takes shelter in the temple ruin that she claims as belonging to her. She finds herself intrigued by this stranger who like her, seeks the solitude of the forest. The stranger maintains his anonymity, but demonstrates acceptance and appreciation of her personality, which is contrary to her expectations. He expresses a genuine interest in knowing her and encourages her to talk about herself. He overlooks her eccentricity and labels her interesting and brilliant. For the first time in her life, *Ammini* meets a person who finds something of value in her. The stranger gifts her a book on birds- a hobby she is passionate about. *Ammini* is comfortable in his companionship, but she does not develop any psychological dependence on this relationship. She is grateful to the stranger, but has no expectations of him.

***Devan** plays the stranger that **Ammini** meets in the course of her wanderings in the forest*

Mohan, a sociology student and a family friend, visits *Ammini's* family with his parents. *Mohan's* family is wealthy and owns a large share of the estate. *Shylaja's* parents have a vested interest in *Mohan-* they aspire to give him their daughter's hand in marriage. Though *Mohan* is friendly to *Shylaja*, he has no romantic interest in her. Instead, *Mohan* falls in love with *Ammini's* personality. He is drawn to the beauty of her spirit. He celebrates her eccentricity and sees through it. He gently uncovers her masks of defence, exposing the feminine spirit she guards within. Demonstrating his feelings for her, he passionately kisses her, transforming her world. *Mohan's* love awakens the woman in her. Her womanhood finally summons the courage to step out into the world. This phase explores the impact of love on personality. The scar of parental rejection is put to rest.

Ammini transforms as an individual. Eccentricity and loudness give way to a tranquil silence. In this tranquillity, the flowers of womanhood bloom. The song **'Athmavil Muttivillichadu Pole'** (*the feel of someone knocking at the doors of my soul*) breathes life into the awakening of her feminine spirit. *Ammini* is overwhelmed by the awakening of these dormant emotions that give new meaning to her solitary life. She explores these emotions in silence and savours them in solitude.

Vineeth as 'Mohan'- the man who awakens Ammini's feminine spirit

Ammini does not let herself be carried away, unlike *Shylaja* who is impatient, restless and anxious in her love. *Ammini* savours the companionship- her very first feel of intimacy. Her emotions are raw, and bear none of the conditioning that is characteristic of convention. *Shylaja*, on the contrary, is inclined towards giving her interest in *Mohan* a social dimension, and demonstrates impatience with regard to the marriage. The film thus addresses how individuals differ with regard to their psychological needs.

The secure world that Shylaja has always known conditions her to look at relationships from the perspective of social security. Marriage represents that security. However, Ammini has never known emotional security as an individual. The lack of love and companionship in her early life seed in her a need for warmth, intimacy and companionship. She revels in the fulfilment of these needs in her companionship with Mohan and celebrates the companionship. While Shylaja weaves dreams into a distant future, Ammini celebrates the present.

Just as *Ammini* starts to celebrate her newfound love, fate intervenes and tragedy strikes. *Mohan* is killed in a communal attack, putting an abrupt end to all the dreams of her womanhood.

While it would be natural to expect *Ammini* to break down irreparably, *Ammini* surprises us with the resilience of her spirit. *Shylaja*, whose relationship with *Mohan* has never really seen the light of dawn, is devastated by *Mohan's* death. But *Ammini*, to whom *Mohan* has proclaimed his love and commitment, demonstrates her ability to come to terms with his death. She consoles *Shylaja*, never once revealing the bleeding of her own spirit.

Parvathy as the disapproving 'Shylaja'

She turns to the forests for sharing this loss- to their undying and unconditional companionship. She takes respite in her abode in the temple ruins and pours out her sorrow into her notebook.

The strength of her personality evolves in her final act, wherein she tends to *Mohan's* murderer- the stranger whom she had befriended in the forest, as she understands the social context in which he committed the act, and helps him escape. But the police shoot him down in the climax of the film.

Ammini loses both the people who have given her love and filled the void in her solitary life, but that doesn't kill the music in her soul. True to the words she once scribbled in her notebook, *Ammini's* autobiography emerges more courageous than that of *Madhavikutty's* '***Ente katha***'!

Ammini is shocked by the revelation that the stranger is the cause of Mohan's death.

'Aranyakam' narrates the story of a vulnerable woman who confronts trauma early in life, and is in acceptance of it. The film takes us through the adaptive defense mechanisms that integrate into her personality and allow its successful expression. The film celebrates the vulnerability of her spirit and illustrates how the most vulnerable of human beings can demonstrate a potential for resilience. The film highlights the significance of acceptance in the art of survival.

Uᴅʏᴀɴᴀᴘᴀʟᴀᴋᴀɴ

Lohithadas's characters have always been ingrained in the tradition and culture of Kerala. His characters were largely simple village folk borrowed from the real life characters that dotted the landscape of Indian villages- characters that defined the traditional Indian spirit:

Individuals with simple exteriors, but profound souls.

The simplicity and modesty that masked the profundity of their souls, the resilience that masked their vulnerability, the profound ability to love that masked the loveless void in their own lives- these aspects of his characters endeared them to the common man and made them immensely lovable.

The lack of such characters is palpable in modern day cinema. So is the richness of script that breathed life into his characters and endowed them profound depth. *Lohithadas*'s script was his signature. He had that unique ability of packing the deep philosophical essence of life into the simplicity of language. His script formed the soul of his films.

Through his script, Lohithadas introduced us to the inspirational characters that defined raw human nature, bringing to visibility the infinite layers beneath which a soul throbbed and gleamed in all its beauty.

Lohithadas with director **Bharathan** and cinematographer **Ramachandra Babu** at the location of *'Venkalam'*

Sudhakaran Nair in Udyanapalakan[70] is one such character.

His kinship with gardens and the deep meaning he derives from this role is the central theme of this film.

Mammootty *as the vulnerable Sudhakaran Nair in* **Udyanapalakan**

The film introduces **Ammu**, the pampered granddaughter of *K G Menon* (*Oduvil Unnikrishnan*), a respectable figure in the village.

Ammu is independent, adventurous, bubbly and full of childish mischief. She is impulsive, restless and seeks persistent excitement. Her pranks are reflections of this persistent need for excitement. One is led to believe that *Ammu*'s world is resplendent with the love of her grandparents and the comforts that money can buy. However, *Ammu*'s sensation-seeking behaviour reflects in reality the emotional void in her life that she carefully conceals beneath her mischievous and adventurous spirit. The mischief and extraversion help her cope with the emptiness that she feels in the absence of parental love.

It is the void created by her unfulfilled need for intimacy and companionship that Ammu attempts to escape by this sensation-seeking behaviour. Her grandparents and her family members fail to recognize this vulnerability.

Sudhakaran Nair is a patriotic ex-military *jawan* who has injured his leg in a war and therefore limps as he walks. He is obsessed with gardens. His garden represents to him a work of art for it is the outcome of his creativity and perseverance. He views his garden as an aesthetic world created with deep love, care and imagination. To *Sudhakaran Nair*, his garden is a world with a soul- a world whose integrity is not to be disturbed. The deep meaning he derives from his kinship with his garden is illustrated in his words to *Ammu*:

"There is a joy in planting a stem-cutting; in witnessing the sprouting of new life from it; in nurturing it and watching it grow into a healthy plant that flowers and fruits. The joy of witnessing each milestone of the plant can never be obtained from artificial flowers."

Kaveri as the mischievous and impulsive Ammu

Lohithadas draws an important inference in his script:

Happiness lies in the journey and not in the outcome per se. It is only happiness that is erected on a journey of effort, struggle and pain that is capable of nourishing the soul.

To *Sudhakaran Nair*, the flowers in his garden are extensions of his soul, and he is immensely pained when the villagers steal his flowers or request him for flowers on the occasion of weddings and funerals. The children humour themselves by stealing flowers from his garden and mocking his limp.

But to Sudhakaran Nair, the flower is rooted into its mother plant in an inseparable bonding- one that is painful to severe.

To the simple minds of the village folk, *Sudhakaran Nair's* passion is an eccentricity. Yet, the landscape of rural life accommodates this eccentricity with ease. The film introduces numerous characters who are an integral and inseparable part of his life. *Lohithadas* paints a sensitive picture of human relationships, devoid of any sentimentality. He retains the sublime tone of human relationships that mimics life and thus brings realism into the film.

> *Lohithadas's characters lack stereotypy and perfection; his characters are a concoction of positive and negative traits that define raw human nature. Lohithadas portrays human behaviour as an outcome of differing motivational drives, influenced by fundamental traits that rest on a foundation of traditional values. His characters demonstrate beneath all their shrewdness and imperfections a fundamental goodness that is inherent to human nature.*

Sudhakaran Nair is a principled man. Yet, his mind accommodates the unfairness and insensitivity of the world. Beneath the external façade of strength that he puts up, *Sudhakaran Nair* guards a vulnerable mind. His mother, his younger sister *Suma* and his companion *Gopalan (Nedumudi Venu)*, recognize this vulnerability. They demonstrate a deep concern for him and this forms the basis of his intimate relationship with these individuals.

The invisible thread of emotions that bind human beings into mutual interdependence is portrayed with sensitivity.

Lakshmi Krishnamurthy *plays the role of Sudhakaran Nair's mother*

On the contrary, the rest of his family members do not understand his need for empathy, care and concern.

At a young age, *Sudhakaran Nair* is thrust into the role of a breadwinner. He joins the Army and endures the tough life of a *jawan* in order to cater to the financial needs of his siblings. He marries off his siblings and secures their lives. But when he finally completes his tenure and returns to his village, the older siblings show no concern towards his life.

They fail to acknowledge the hardships that have gone into the moulding of his vulnerable spirit into one adept at survival. They fail to acknowledge the sacrifices he has made towards securing their lives. They take for granted his parental role in their lives in the absence of a father figure. They label him as egotistic and impractical.

They fail to see his need for love and care and view him as a self-sufficient and self-reliant individual who is capable of independently taking care of his needs.

Sudhakaran Nair is deeply hurt by this insensitivity. However, his self-worth prevents him from exposing this vulnerability.

The plot now focuses on the relationship between *Sudhakaran Nair* and *Ammu*.

Ammu's immature character and impulsivity contrast sharply with *Sudhakaran Nair*'s maturity and thoughtfulness. While *Ammu* is well-to-do, pampered and cared for, *Sudhakaran Nair* comes across as a man shaped by his hardships. Despite the differences, life binds them into a relationship born out of unfulfilled emotional needs.

Ammu is bitten by a cobra while she attempts to steal flowers from *Sudhakaran Nair*'s prized garden. *Sudhakaran Nair*'s response to her predicament changes her perspective of him. He demonstrates intense concern for her well-being. While her grandparents break down, *Sudhakaran Nair* shoulders the responsibility of *Ammu*'s hospitalization and care and supports the family through the entire event. *Ammu*'s cousin, *Ram Mohan* (to whom her marriage has long been fixed), does not bring the sensitivity into his reaction that *Ammu*'s vulnerable spirit desires. *Ammu* finds herself drawn to *Sudhakaran Nair* and begins to see him in new light.

Ammu falls in love with his ability to put the vulnerability and need of others above his own vulnerability and needs. Ammu's vulnerability therefore attaches itself to Sudhakaran Nair's potential for love.

Biju Menon *as Dr Ram Mohan, Ammu's cousin*

Remorseful of the pranks she has played on him in the past, *Ammu* sends a cartload of flowering plants to compensate for all the flowers she has stolen from his garden. But *Sudhakaran Nair's* remark renders her speechless:

'*Nothing is ever a substitute for anything.*'

When she apologizes for having ridiculed him in the past, *Sudhakaran Nair's* reply is matter-of-fact:

'*Who doesn't make fun of me?*,' he laughs.

His modesty, altruism and his acceptance of the equation of his life moves *Ammu.*

The emotional void in her own life makes her appreciate the abundance in Sudhakaran Nair's personality.

Ammu reforms as an individual. Mischief and immaturity give way to mellow maturity and tranquillity. Plagued by remorse and guilt over her behaviour in the past, *Ammu* decides to create a garden in the premises of her house. Though this act is initially her means of expressing repentance, she discovers the joy in the process as she indulges in it. *Ammu* follows *Sudhakaran Nair's* example and realizes that true happiness lies in meaningful endeavours. She learns to differentiate between the transience of pleasure and the permanence of happiness. Her subsequent behaviour is driven by her deep regard for *Sudhakaran Nair*.

The film takes a turn as *Ammu* confesses her love for *Sudhakaran Nair*. His age, his limp and his eccentricity become immaterial to her. *Ammu* finds in his companionship a reassurance that she has never felt before. The deep emotional void that lies beneath her high-spiritedness is revealed in her words:

"A tree in full bloom- that is your love. As I stand beneath this tree, I feel none of the pain that characterizes my life. There is only bliss here.

It is not a handsome fool that I need in marriage. I am in need of a father's affection, a brother's companionship, a husband's security and a lover's playful innocence."

Sudhakaran Nair also transforms under the influence of his relationship with *Ammu*. Stability gives way to emotional lability and impulsivity. He begins to reciprocate to *Ammu*'s emotions, and overlooks the differences that come in the way of the feasibility of their relationship. He becomes oblivious to the socioeconomic differences between them, the significant age difference between them, and to all the other factors that lack feasibility in a social context. He is only driven by his need for companionship and by *Ammu*'s insight into his personality. This is contrary to his basic nature.

The film therefore illustrates how impulsivity is often rooted in vulnerability.

Sudhakaran Nair decides to marry *Ammu*, knowing well that her family would never comply with this decision. It is only when *Ram Mohan* reminds him that these differences will surface as time goes by and *Ammu* confronts the reality of his life that *Sudhakaran Nair* awakens to reality. At this point, he finds himself in deep conflict:

While their love for each other is sincere and caters to their emotional needs, will it exhaust itself as time goes by, and Ammu comes in closer contact with the reality of his life?

Will one void abate only to be replaced by another?

He resolves this conflict by making a decision that takes into consideration the emotions of all the people involved in the conflict. *Sudhakaran Nair* refuses to put his suffering over and above the anguish of the people who are close to *Ammu*. He demonstrates sensitivity to their feelings and interests and considers *Ammu*'s impulsivity. He comes to the conclusion that their happiness lies in sacrificing the relationship. His altruism helps him overcome his pain and sacrifice his love.

Sudhakaran Nair empathetically explains his perspective to *Ammu*. He makes it clear that the decision of stepping out does not negate the truth in his love.

With a bleeding spirit, *Sudhakaran Nair* gifts *Ammu* a rose that he has plucked from his garden and parts with the following words:

'This is not just a flower; this is my soul. Preserve it. Like my life, the petals will wither away. But its essence shall remain. You must carry the memory of that essence into your next life.

All our lives have a purpose. Perhaps my purpose in this life is to be a caretaker of gardens. Perhaps your purpose in this life is to be happily married to that young doctor and earn name and fame.'

The climax is the strength of this film. *Sudhakaran Nair* does not end up with depression or rebellion. Despite his vulnerability and deep affinity for *Ammu*, he is able to overcome his pain and move on. He does not lose his motivation in life. This is because he has discovered the true meaning of his life in his kinship with gardens. His motivation from this role is his deepest motivation and this awareness helps him pull through all the traumatic events in his life.

Through the character of *Sudhakaran Nair*, *Lohithadas* sketches an ordinary character who is extraordinary in his perspective of life. The film awakens us to the realization that the most ordinary and simplest of human beings may demonstrate a strong inclination to spirituality and may form strong references portraying self-actualization.

On that note, Lohithadas leaves us with the fragrant memory of a film that teaches us to surpass our stories of vulnerability and unfulfilled dreams by discovering the true meaning of our lives.

CHILLU: BREATHING LIFE INTO BORDERLINE PERSONALITY DISORDER

Chillu...

A piece of glass that is sturdy and firm on the exterior, but so delicate and fragile on the inside that it could break into a million pieces at the slightest trauma.

*Such is the central character of this film[103], **Annie**.*

Annie is a young girl who has lost her mother in childhood and is raised by her father. Her father is more of a companion to her- gentle and liberal, abstaining from criticism. However, the absence of a mother figure in her life seeds in her feelings of insecurity with regard to self-worth. *Annie* guards a fragile self-esteem and is vulnerable. However, she is defensive and attempts to conceal her vulnerability, demonstrating on the exterior a very carefree persona.

Annie's world is small and largely confined to her college campus. Though she is extraverted, *Annie* is not ambitious. She seems to have no specific plans with regard to her future. *Annie* surrounds herself with people. Her day-to-day life revolves around her jovial conversations with her father, her intellectual conversations with her classmate *Ananthu*, her interactions with her cousin *Manu* and his family. She is uncomfortable with solitude; she tries to escape her solitary moments by surrounding herself with people or by engaging in idle telephonic conversations with Manu.

Despite her extraversion, there is a stillness and silence in *Annie's* personality that reflects a deep emotional void that she persistently fills with her relationships. It is as if *Annie's* extraversion is a defence born out of a need to escape the emotional void that she refuses to confront. However, her casual approach to her relationships with people almost conceals the deep meaning she derives from relationships.

Annie is impulsive and volatile. There is a restlessness about her that causes her to seek persistent change in her environment. One moment, she is seen engaging in casual banter with her friends in the college campus. The next moment, she is seen drifting to an intellectual engagement with *Ananthu*. Her restlessness then drives her to seek the emotional intimacy that *Manu's* companionship provides.

Annie switches from one interaction to the other, yet fails to be grounded.

She is also confused about her relationships. She fails to define them on concrete terms. When asked if she is in love with *Manu*, her answer illustrates her confusion:

'I feel restless if I don't get to see him in the course of a day. Is that love?'

In truth, this reflects the insecurity that colours her feelings of love. It reflects her emotional lability and her dependence on relationships. She laughs at her answer and one is led to believe that *Annie* is self-reliant and autonomous. But in truth, the laughter is a sublimation defense that conceals her dependence.

Annie's restlessness and confusion is a reflection of the fragile self-esteem and sense of worthlessness that she has never outgrown. This causes her to be overly dependent on relationships as a source of positive regard.

***Shanthi Krishna** plays the fragile 'Annie' in Lenin Rajendran's 'Chillu'*

Annie's fragile self-esteem is nourished by the need people demonstrate towards her presence in their lives. She derives a sense of worth when people seek her companionship. *Ananthu* sees in her an intellectual companion and this makes her feel worthy and valued. *Manu* has been a part of her life since her childhood. He is as habituated to her presence in his life as she is to his companionship. *Manu's* companionship gives her a sense of purpose and nourishes her fragile self-esteem. While her relationships are in place, *Annie* is idealistic, joyful and loving. However, her fundamental insecurity with regard to her feelings of worthlessness manifests as an unvoiced fear of rejection. Annie conceals this fear and portrays quite the opposite in the volatility that characterizes her personality.

In truth, it is her fear of rejection that manifests as her volatility and inability to commit.

Annie's inability to define her relationships on concrete terms and her inclination towards *Ananthu* makes *Manu* insecure. He fails to be convinced of her ability to commit and his insecurity causes him to seek a new companionship in his cousin *Lali*. Though this new association is born out of mere impulsivity and the need to make *Annie* feel insecure, *Manu's* mother intervenes in their relationship. She feels disturbed and concerned by *Manu's* insecurity as she realizes that *Annie's* personality will be a persistent source of insecurity to *Manu*. She advises *Annie* to step back from the relationship.

Rony Vincent *plays the insecure 'Manu' in **Chillu***

Annie breaks down and her fragility surfaces. Her vitality is replaced by a brooding personality – a personality that is overwhelmed by the pain of rejection and abandonment. Her feelings of worthlessness refuse to abate and brew into depression. She experiences mood swings and emotional instability. One moment, she is seen crying out loud and the next moment, she gathers herself up, ignoring the deep heartache that is gnawing at her.

She switches from vulnerability to defence and back to vulnerability.

Depression turns into a season that refuses to leave. Her mind desperately seeks an escape route. On an impulse, she visits *Ananthu*. Their college life has come to an end and *Ananthu* is leaving. Her mind desperately longs to hold on to someone who will comfort her and help her tide over her depression. She expresses her desire to accompany *Ananthu*, merely to escape from the emotional chaos within her mind. This reflects her inability to cope with the loss on her own.

She seeks the security of one relationship to be able to cope with the loss of another.

This illustrates the fact that her relationships are primarily driven by her intense need for positive regard. However, when Ananthu expresses his helplessness, she is quick to repress the vulnerability she has transiently exposed. Annie now comes face to face with her loneliness. This unmasks the raw Annie who is intensely dependent on her relationships for happiness.

Venu Nagavally *plays the melancholic and contemplative 'Ananthu'*

Manu's wedding with *Lali* is fixed. *Annie* attends *Manu's* wedding. She plays the perfect host to the guests, her face belying the chaos within.

She is highly defensive for she refuses to reveal her vulnerability to *Manu* and his family. She feigns detachment and attends to the guests. However, she is unable to hold up her defence for long and she bursts into tears.

Annie is unable to cope with the loneliness and emptiness. The fact that *Manu* and *Ananthu* are able to move on and cope with her absence in their lives, creates feelings of intense worthlessness in her mind. In the absence of a higher meaning in her life, *Annie* is unable to tide over this loss. Unable to cope with the anxiety and deep conflict, *Annie* resorts to suicide. Like a human being who would rather jump out of the window of a high-rise apartment that catches fire and die than endure the flames, *Annie* prefers suicide to the negativity of her emotions. That is her final impulsive act.

> *Through the character of Annie, 'Chillu' opens the windows of our mind to the entity of borderline personality disorder. The film sheds light on the internal journey of the fragile spirit that lies at the heart of this disorder. It sensitizes us to the underlying emotional needs of such a personality and enables us to read beneath the external defences put up by these individuals. It teaches us to be responsible in our relationships, emphasizing on the importance of sensitivity, empathy, care and concern in our relationships with people.*

ULLADAKKAM: A PORTRAYAL OF POST TRAUMATIC STRESS DISORDER

If we were to chart the journey of our minds, we would realize that the paths available for it are infinite and uncharted. The mind ventures through these paths untrammelled, and when we have travelled too far in this maze, we find ourselves lost. A certain fear grips us for we no longer know the way out or the way back. We find ourselves surrounded by unfamiliarity and uncertainty.

This is how the film[98] unfolds. A dream, wherein **Dr Sunny**, a psychiatrist by profession, finds himself trapped in such a maze and wakes up in distress. The dream is symbolic of our powerlessness over our own minds. This fact is subsequently reflected by *Dr Sunny*:

'Our minds are far beyond us. They cannot be contained by the logic of our thoughts.'

Mohanlal plays the pensive 'Dr Sunny' in Ulladakkam

The film introduces us to a composed and reflective *Dr Sunny* who demonstrates a personal interest in treating his patient **Reshma** who is his best friend's sister. *Reshma* is reported to be reacting aggressively and abnormally.

Sunny is led to *Reshma*'s room, where he catches a glimpse of *Reshma* crouching in a corner in a highly agitated state. The room is in shambles. *Reshma* demonstrates hypervigilance to her environment and reacts violently to *Sunny*'s approach towards her.

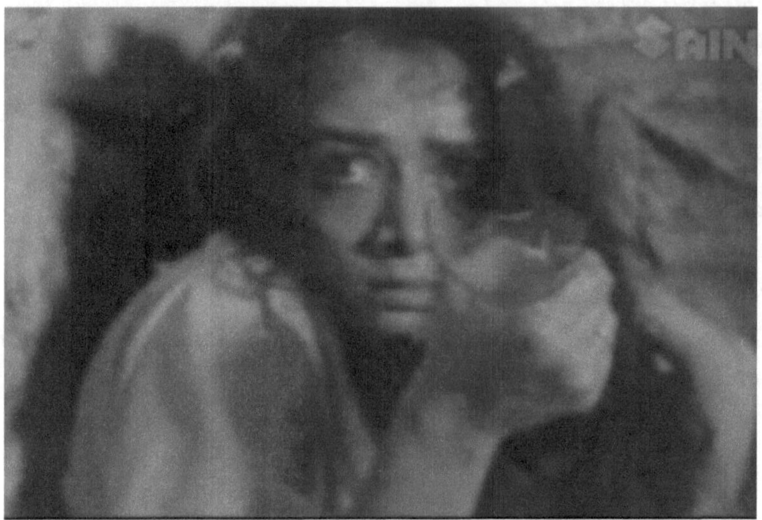

Amala Akkineni as 'Reshma' in ***Ulladakkam***

Sunny arranges for *Reshma* to be shifted to the hospital. As she is taken to the hospital, she appears less agitated, but has a vacant expression that is suggestive of dissociation. She demonstrates no interest in her surroundings and appears to have lost touch with reality. She is put on tranquilizers and sedated. Meanwhile, *Sunny* probes into her background. He discovers a few clues in her diary. Her deep vulnerability is exposed in her ramblings. There are imaginary letters written to her deceased mother. *Sunny* learns from her brother that as a child, *Reshma* had reacted violently to her mother's death and that was her first psychotic episode. *Sunny* learns that the episode was transient and had resolved completely.

Sunny explores the trigger for the current psychotic episode. From the *Rorschach cards* he displays to her, he gathers that the current trauma has an association with the sea for *Reshma* becomes highly agitated when he shows her the imagery on a card that is reminiscent of the sea.

The film illustrates the strength of associative memory in such a personality. Reshma reacts aggressively to any factor that bears an association with the trauma- places, people, objects. The images of the event are vivid in her mind. Any component in that association triggers in her a strong memory of the trauma that she continues to resist.

With further clues, *Sunny* comes to the conclusion that the trauma pertains to the mysterious disappearance of her boyfriend, *Arun*. He subjects *Reshma* to hypnosis and manages to elicit the story of *Arun's* death. *Reshma* reveals the details of *Arun's* brutal murder by a mafia gang on that fateful day as they had been conversing at the beach, unsuspecting of the tragedy that was to unfold. As she re-experiences the trauma of the event in her mind, the memory of *Arun* being beaten up and his body being washed away into the sea causes much agitation and turbulence in her.

Sunny gathers that *Reshma* is resisting the reality of the trauma and that her psychotic episode is rooted in her inability to overcome her denial. Her unconscious protects her vulnerability by resisting the unpleasant event. It is this resistance and repression that is reflected in the title of the film, **Ulladakkam**.

Sunny makes attempts to break her resistance by helping her relive the trauma in her mind so as to be able to internalize it. *Reshma* is made to narrate the event. The narration constitutes a form of **exposure therapy** wherein the therapist provides a supportive environment that helps her relive the trauma in her mind and come to terms with it. She is also given a guarded exposure to the sea- an important object in her mental imagery of the trauma. He succeeds in helping her rid herself of the sea phobia.

***Therapy** for this disorder is essentially cognitive therapy and exposure therapy. The film focuses on **exposure therapy** (helping the patient re-experience the event in real or imaginary terms so that they lose phobia for the components of the memory).*[65]

Reshma gradually recovers from her dissociation and allows her mind to feel the unpleasant emotions associated with the traumatic event. But she does so with the aid of ***transference***- the unconscious redirection of emotions from the deceased *Arun* to a new person:

She develops a special bonding with one of the inmates- an elderly lady (Sukumari) who demonstrates affection towards her. Reshma sees in her a mother figure and demonstrates transference towards her. However, just as Reshma begins to find reassurance in her companionship, the elderly lady is discharged from the asylum.

This devastates Reshma. Her mind desperately seeks a new outlet for her repressed emotions, and she directs her transference towards Dr Sunny whose warmth and care replicate the emotional fulfilment she had derived from her relationship with Arun.

Reshma demonstrates an emotional dependence on *Dr Sunny* and is oblivious to the social implications of such attachment. She demonstrates a lack of sensitivity towards his responsibilities and his social engagements, including his relationship with *Annie* whom he intends to marry. This contradicts her fundamental empathetic and selfless nature.

Sunny finds himself in conflict as *Reshma* demonstrates overt dependence on him, and he attempts to withdraw from his association with her. But his attempts at withdrawal are perceived as serious threats by *Reshma's* mind that is now dangerously dependent on *Sunny's* persistent attention. She attempts suicide in response to his withdrawal.

Just as *Sunny* and *Annie* decide to postpone their wedding on account of *Reshma's* unresolved conflict, *Reshma* discovers the truth of the circumstances and becomes aware of the complications she is causing unknowingly. This breaks the bubble in her mind and brings to light the distress she has caused *Dr Sunny*, *Annie* and their family members. *Reshma* is deeply hurt by the manner in which her behaviour is perceived by them. She is unable to accept the fact that they resent her behaviour. Driven by the need to protect her self-esteem, *Reshma* makes a conscious effort to detach from *Dr Sunny*. She succeeds (at the expense of the repressed emotions that are still seeking an outlet). Much to the relief of the family members, she withdraws from *Dr Sunny's* life, liberating him from his distressful predicament.

The film takes a final twist on the occasion of *Sunny's* wedding reception, when *Reshma* finds her repressed emotions evoked by the sight of the percussionists in the band. Her mind associates this image with *Arun*, causing the unresolved trauma of his death to resurface. The deep anxiety thus created manifests as an acute episode of dissociation and agitation. *Reshma* becomes hypervigilant and this causes her to murder *Annie* as an unsuspecting *Annie* follows the dissociated *Reshma* and attempts to calm her.

The film illustrates the fact that though Reshma is cured of her phobia with regard to the event of Arun's brutal murder, she remains in denial of the loss of Arun's companionship. Her mind continues to resist this fact, and any stimulus which is a reminder of this loss, sets off the psychosis. True to the nature of 'Post Traumatic Stress Disorder,' Arun's death is an ongoing event in her mind, and not an event of the past.

Shobhana *as 'Annie'- the victim of Reshma's psychosis*

The film sensitively paints a picture of 'Post Traumatic Stress Disorder' through the character sketch of Reshma. It illuminates the deep emotional void that is at the heart of this disorder and that forms the basis of the denial, dissociation and dependence that may characterize such a personality.

Innale: Exploring Dissociative Amnesia

"Memory is the diary that we all carry about us."

- Oscar Wilde

Who are we?

Are we the accumulated residues of our pasts…our yesterdays?

Are we defined by the family and friends we have spent time with, the social and professional roles we have played, the places we have inhabited, and everything else that we hold in conscious memory?

If memories define us, then who are we, in the absence of those memories?

Through the plot of this film[106], *Padmarajan* successfully shakes the very foundation of our beliefs pertaining to our identity in the mortal world. We find ourselves transported to that thin line that separates fact and fiction, life and existence. The film opens our eyes to the fact that the only footprints we leave behind in this mortal life are the memories we create in the minds of the people we have touched. These memories are the only proof of our existence-the only proof of moments that have transpired.

The film unfolds with disturbing scenes of rescue operations following a bus accident in a remote village on hilly terrain. As victims are taken to the only private hospital in the village and successively pronounced dead after futile attempts at restoring their lives, we are introduced to a middle-aged *Dr Sandhya*, who looks at her blood-stained hands and sighs in despair.

Dr Sandhya is a dedicated doctor who runs a hospital in the village (property she has inherited from her deceased father), with the assistance of her son, *Sharath*. *Sharath*, an MBBS drop-out, is the manager of the hospital. Just as they believe they are through with the victims of the accident, a young girl whose body is discovered further downstream by some villagers, is brought to the hospital in a comatose state. *Dr Sandhya* and her team manage to save her life.

Srividya as 'Dr Sandhya' in **Innale**

The very first glimpse of this young girl is shrouded in mystery. As she lies in coma in a hospital bed that is alien to her being, blissfully unaware of the deep tragedy that has befallen her, we find ourselves haunted by a series of unanswered questions.

Who is she? Somebody's daughter, perhaps. Or somebody's wife. Where is she from? Where was she going to? Is there somebody anxiously awaiting her?

As these questions haunt us, we watch the young girl slip in and out of coma- in and out of spells of deep sleep. Eventually, when she wakes up to reality, it is to discover that she remembers nothing of her past.

Not even her name.

In the course of our carefully woven lives, none of us would perhaps imagine such a scenario. A scenario wherein we woke up one day with no memory of our past. Not even a memory of the name that defined us until yesterday. No memory of the faces that were a part of our lives until yesterday. No memory of a home that we inhabited until yesterday.

No memory of all the memories we formed until yesterday- the yesterdays that defined us.

*Maya (**Shobhana**) is in turmoil as she recollects nothing of her past*

The young girl is in turmoil. As she desperately tries to unveil the mist that blankets her past, hoping that she might discover some imprint of that past in the vestiges of her mind, *Dr Sandhya* and *Sharath* watch helplessly. Desperation and recurring nightmares give way to hopelessness and mute silence.

A consultation with the psychiatrist puts an end to this quest for a memory trace:

> *'A case of hysterical amnesia. Rather disturbing, but nevertheless, leaving behind all the learnt skills intact. The memory loss predominantly involves people, places and events. However, if you have learnt a language, you will retain that ability. If you have learnt music, you will retain the ability to sing. You will know what a cinema is, but you will be unable to recall a single film that you have watched. You are a normal person for your cognitive ability is intact. You should find your strength in that. Look at the amnesia as the price you had to pay for coming out alive from a major accident. You must now accept this as your reality and come to terms with it.'*

Sharath finds a name for her.

'*Maya.* I like the name. It suits my current predicament.' she responds.

Sharath advises her:

'*You have no access to your past. That being the case, think of your past as something that no longer belongs to you. It belongs to a different Maya. Instead of trying to gather fragments from a life that has passed and that no longer belongs to you, embrace the life that lies ahead of you and that belongs to you.*'

Jayaram *as the impulsive and labile '*Sharath*' in* ***Innale***

Padmarajan's character *Maya* is a beautiful young girl. This makes the predicament more challenging on account of the safety issues that she must face. With nowhere to go, and with several opportunistic men waiting to take advantage of her predicament, *Maya* is saved from further anxiety by *Dr Sandhya* and *Sharath*, who take a humanitarian stand and decide to keep her under their protection until the time a guardian rightfully claims her.

Maya is moved from the hospital to a little house that belongs to *Dr Sandhya*, and an elderly lady, *Rahelamma* is appointed for her care. *Maya* is also appointed as a teacher in a primary school owned by *Dr Sandhya*. *Maya* now starts building a new life-

A life severed from its yesterdays.

The palpable solitude of the village and the background music sensitize us to *Maya's* predicament. The trees, birds and the breeze bring with them the fragrance of an unknown nostalgic memory from a distant past- a past that is no longer accessible to *Maya*. The song '***Kannil Nin Meyyil***,' explores *Maya's* predicament as it poetically describes her perception in the light of lost memories.

As *Maya* slowly builds a new life with the support of *Dr Sandhya* and *Sharath*, she takes a liking to *Sharath*. *Sharath* and *Maya* fall in love and despite the anxiety pertaining to *Maya's* unrevealed past, *Dr Sandhya* finally consents and formally announces their wedding.

The film takes a twist with the entry of *Dr Narendran* on the scene. *Narendran*, a PhD holder in Physics, arrives in Bombay, to investigate the missing of his wife, *Gowri*. The film subsequently takes us through *Narendran's* memory of *Gowri*- of their first encounter, of their courtship and quiet wedding, of their brief life of blissful togetherness, and of their subsequent parting as *Narendran* leaves to the United States. He recollects *Gowri's* zealous tone when she had discussed her plans of a pilgrimage trip to South India- an opportunity to step into a land to which she belonged, but that she had never visited. An opportunity to thank the Gods for this treasure that life had gifted her after all her years of emptiness. He looks at the postcard that was last posted to him by *Gowri*- a card from *Tirupathi*.

He had not known then that this was the last token from the cherished life he was building with Gowri.

Investigations take *Narendran* to the village where *Gowri* is leading her new life as *Maya*. *Narendran's* arrival on the scene is received by *Sharath* and *Dr Sandhya* with much anxiety and apprehension.

The climax of the film is haunting. As *Narendran* comes face to face with a woman who is *Gowri* in physical appearance, but whose amnesia has erased his face from her mind, *Narendran* finds himself in deep conflict. As he contemplates on the next step, we find ourselves holding our breath.

Narendran stuns us into silence as he puts aside all the evidence he has brought along to prove that *Gowri* is his wife- their wedding photographs, their marriage certificate and all other documentary evidence.

He awakens us to the realization that these physical fragments of evidence are of no value in the absence of memories for memories alone have the ability to breathe life into matter. In the absence of the memories that defined their relationship, these documents are reduced to lifeless bits of paper.

Narendran leaves without revealing the truth, much to *Sharath*'s relief. *Sharath* believes that *Maya* is not the *Gowri* that *Narendran* was looking for, and he celebrates this moment of relief, unaware of the truth, and oblivious to the future.

Suresh Gopi *plays the rational 'Narendran' in* **Innale**

Padmarajan's portrayal of dissociative amnesia is in close alignment to the clinical presentation of this condition. **Dissociative amnesia** *can occur without any structural damage to the brain, as is the case in this film. Maya's brain scans and other tests are reported as normal. Dissociative amnesia often occurs due to a traumatic situation that individuals wish to consciously or unconsciously avoid. As a sensitive young woman who is an orphan, and who has lived a life of emotional void characterized by the absence of family and close companions, Narendran's entry into Maya's life sprouts new life in the arid desert of her mind. The marriage seeds hopes and dreams in the emptiness of her life. It is quite natural for such a personality to experience deep denial towards the trauma that threatens to dismantle a life that she has just begun to weave. Maya's mind therefore rejects the reality of the accident. The onset of dissociative amnesia can be either global, wherein the individual forgets all aspects of the past, or situation specific wherein the individual is unable to retrieve memories of specific situations. In this film, Padmarajan portrays a case of global amnesia, wherein Maya has no memory of her past.*

Maya, true to the clinical manifestation of this condition, easily comes to terms with reality, and begins to accept her new identity.

As is the case with this condition, her memory does not recover from presenting to her information from her past. Memory can be and usually is recovered spontaneously in these individuals.

And that leaves us with the lingering question:

What if she regains her memory of the past? In that event, it is likely that she will be amnesic to the events subsequent to the accident. She will transform into *Gowri*, with no memory of *Maya*, or the elements that defined *Maya*'s life. *Sharath* and *Dr Sandhya*, her saviours and guardians who helped her through a major crisis and gave her new life, will be erased from the reality of her life.

The film therefore emphasizes on the role of the human mind in the perception of reality. It highlights the fact that our minds are far beyond us, and that the reality of our lives is at the mercy of our minds, over which we have little control, contrary to what we commonly assume.

Ennu Swantham Janakikutty: An Exploration Of Dissociative Identity Disorder

'*Yours truly, Janakikutty,*' reads the title of the film.[100]

The film is indeed a journey into the external and internal world of Janakikutty, through her very own eyes. Janakikutty pauses at various junctures in the film to make remarks to herself, as if talking to an invisible spectator. She fantasizes her life as a film that has an invisible audience to whom she constantly communicates.

The film commences with a song sequence that introduces us to the rich perceptive world of *Janakikutty* as she seeks aesthetic stimulation in the course of her wild, aimless strolls through the fields and groves. *Janakikutty* is enchanted by the perceptions that feed her fantasies- reflections of the sun in the water, dragonflies hovering around lotus buds, silky cobwebs gleaming in the sun, the mystic petals of the *Mandaram (Mountain Ebony), water* glistening between the leaves of the water lily, and so much more. In the wilderness, she discovers immense possibility. The lyrics of the song '*Ambili Poovattam Ponnuruli*' breathe life into *Janakikutty*'s world of fantasy.

In her world of fantasy, Janakikutty is the central character around which everything revolves.

Jomol plays the fantasy prone character of 'Janakikutty'

Janakikutty then introduces us to her family members. The household is a conventional matrilineal *Nair Tharavadu* whose women hold on to their traditional roles. We get a glimpse of her mother who is always preoccupied with the household chores and has no time for *Janakikutty*. She then introduces us to her aunt who dotes on her only daughter and spends hours grooming her and dressing her up. Finally, she introduces us to her siblings- a sister obsessed with celebrities and their lives, and an unemployed brother who keeps to himself.

Nobody appears to take notice of Janakikutty. With her thick-rimmed glasses, plain clothes and lack of external embellishments, Janakikutty is considered unattractive and ignored by her siblings and cousin. They refuse to make her a part of their world. They do not let her into their little secrets and largely ignore her. The self-absorbed family members have no time for conversations. This emptiness and loneliness drives Janakikutty to find respite in the outdoors.

This monotony at home is finally broken by the arrival of a distant relative- an elderly lady whose children have abandoned her. She is regarded as an unwelcome guest in the household for she is perceived as a troublemaker. However, *Janakikutty* celebrates her arrival and finds her talkativeness a welcome change. *Janakikutty* calls her *Muthassi* (grandmother).

Janakikutty and Muthassi build a silent bonding, born out of the common factor in both their lives- a sense of loneliness and worthlessness.

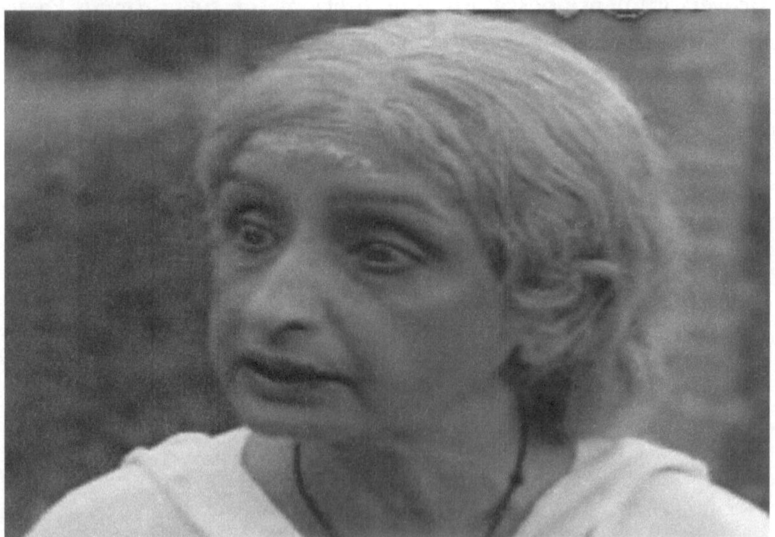

***Valsala Menon** as 'Muthassi,' Janakikutty's sole companion*

The film then introduces *Bhaskaran*, the family's caretaker's son. *Bhaskaran* is the only character who takes notice of *Janakikutty* and demonstrates affection towards her, bringing her little gifts and taking an interest in her perceptions and thoughts. *Bhaskaran* dispels her feelings of worthlessness with regard to her appearance and makes her believe that he is capable of finding beauty in her. *Janakikutty*, who has never regarded her unattractive self as worthy of love, finds this an unbelievable ray of hope in the dark solitude of her life and holds on to the emotion. *Janakikutty's* fragile self-esteem clings desperately to *Bhaskaran's* positive regard. She celebrates her newfound relationship and her fragile mind views the relationship as a lifeline for it is the first time that a person has made her feel worthy. *Bhaskaran* fails to realize the seriousness with which she regards his interest in her, and does not reveal to her his romantic involvement with *Sarojini*, her cousin.

It is spring in Janakikutty's fantasy world for love is in bloom. The song 'Chempakapoo Mottinullil' captures her exhilaration at her newfound love.

***Sharath** as 'Bhaskaran,' Janakikutty's only source of positive regard*

Meanwhile, *Muthassi* narrates folklores and tales that capture *Janakikutty's* attention. She listens with avidity as *Muthassi* narrates to her the legend of a *Yakshi* who is believed to wander in the grove, seeking vengeance against her husband, a *Namboodiri* who was a womanizer and who killed her by drowning her in the well. The *Yakshi*, whom *Muthassi* calls *Kunjathol*, is portrayed as a bloodthirsty spirit with the devil's tooth, and is claimed to be seen by passersby as a beautiful lady who wanders across the grove in white robes, her hair let loose, begging for some tobacco to chew. *Janakikutty's* mind conjures up an image of the *Yakshi*. *Janakikutty* is fascinated by the story of the *Yakshi* and demonstrates an obsession for it.

The *Yakshi* is vivid in *Janakikutty's* imaginative mind, and she supplements the image and adds character to it with the *Yakshi* stories she reads. Thus, her mind breathes life into the character of *Kunjathol*.

One day, *Janakikutty* finds *Bhaskaran* walking across the grove that is believed to be haunted by the *Yakshi*. She follows him to warn him of the potential danger, but meets with shock as she catches sight of him talking to *Sarojini*, and realizes that they are in love. *Janakikutty* is shattered and is unable to come to terms with this reality. She flees in desperation, only to fall and faint. When she wakes up, she is in a state of dissociation. Her mind refuses to dwell upon the trauma and shuts it out. In the dissociated state, she hears her name being called and catches sight of the *Yakshi 'Kunjathol'* approaching her. Her mind fantasizes *Kunjathol* as being very kind and affectionate towards her, and in this fantasy figure who has supernatural powers, *Janakikutty* finds consolation.

Her mind thus distorts reality in order to cope with the trauma.

Chanchal as the Yakshi 'Kunjathol,' the fantasy character in Janakikutty's imaginative mind

When she comes back to her senses, she finds herself at home, surrounded by her family members who inform her that she was found unconscious in the grove. She appears a little disoriented, but as her eyes catch sight of *Sarojini*, there is a palpable transformation in her demeanour. Her facial expression momentarily turns fierce and turbulent, causing *Sarojini* to withdraw in fear.

Later that night, *Janakikutty* passes *Sarojini*'s room and catches sight of her clothes and cosmetics. Her turbulence returns as she recollects the traumatic episode for her mind holds *Sarojini* responsible for the trauma. She continues to resist the unpleasant emotions associated with the trauma and this again triggers an episode of dissociation. In the dissociated state, *Janakikutty* destroys *Sarojini*'s clothes and cosmetics, but fantasizes that this act is done by the more powerful *Kunjathol*.

Kunjathol thus transforms into Janakikutty's saviour. The fantasy character of Kunjathol is created from all that is lacking in Janakikutty. Janakikutty's mind views Kunjathol as the solution to all her weaknesses- her vulnerability, helplessness, passivism and her inability to exert control on her environment to meet her needs.

The episodes of dissociation and fantasy are recurrent, and the shift is so spontaneous and effortless that one almost fails to recognize the transition between the two identities. The orthodox family members resort to black magic in order to rid *Janakikutty* of the spirit they believe has possessed her. As the rituals proceed in the belief that the spirit will be nailed to a stone, *Janakikutty* imagines *Kunjathol* being nailed to the stone. She protests and screams and this is interpreted by the orthodox audience as the spirit expressing resistance to leave the body.

Janakikutty in a moment of dissociation

The film takes a turn as *Sarojini's* wedding is fixed by her parents. *Sarojini* lacks the courage to oppose the wedding and declare her commitment to *Bhaskaran*. She is pained, but she gives in to the pressure of the family members. *Janakikutty* is unable to rationalize *Sarojini's* reaction to the wedding. She finds it strange that *Sarojini* and *Bhaskaran* are able to call off their relationship so easily.

'The girl states to the boy that there is no way out. The boy sighs and wishes her the very best in life ahead. Is that all there is to love?' *Janakikutty* asks in amusement.

The film thus draws a sharp contrast between the characters of Sarojini and Janakikutty. Sarojini is able to come to acceptance of the loss of a relationship in which she and Bhaskaran had spent intimate moments together. But Janakikutty is deeply devastated by the loss of a relationship that had only been a mirage. While Sarojini sheds tears and moves on, Janakikutty refuses to come to terms with the loss and distorts reality in order to cope with it. This reflects the fragility of her mind and the intensity with which it therefore attaches itself to Bhaskaran's positive regard.

Janakikutty finds it morally wrong that two people in love must give up their love in order to oblige society and convention. She is in denial of this fact for it is an unspoken reminder of her own inability at controlling her environment to meet her needs.

Janakikutty assumes a sense of control as she fantasizes that *Kunjathol* can solve this problem and ensure that *Sarojini* gets married to *Bhaskaran*. She also reassures the bed-ridden *Muthassi* that *Kunjathol's* supernatural powers will enable her to participate in the wedding. The night before the wedding, *Muthassi* passes away. The elders of the family keep this a secret and *Janakikutty* is unaware of this event.

On the day of the wedding, her siblings advise her not to attend the wedding on account of her mental illness. *Janakikutty* is deeply wounded by these statements and decides to stay back. She walks to the haunted grove and holds an imaginary conversation with *Kunjathol*. *Kunjathol* remains passive and takes no steps to stop *Sarojini's* wedding. She states that this wedding is *Sarojini's* fate and that *Bhaskaran* might look at *Janakikutty* differently now that *Sarojini* is married.

Kunjathol's passivism perhaps represents Janakikutty's slow reconciliation with the trauma now that Sarojini has moved on.

Janakikutty decides to get a glimpse of the wedding ceremony. She runs to the house and rushes to *Muthassi's* room. When the caretaker reveals to her that *Muthassi* is dead, *Janakikutty* refuses to believe this information despite the fact that *Muthassi's* limp body lies in front of her eyes. She fantasizes *Muthassi* awakening as a result of *Kunjathol's* supernatural powers and watches her get out of bed. *Janakikutty*, *Muthassi* and *Kunjathol* rush to the temple premises to watch the wedding. As the groom ties the knot, *Janakikutty* witnesses the aggressive transformation of *Kunjathol*. *Janakikutty* is frightened by the devilish teeth that pop out of *Kunjathol's* mouth and by her fierce demeanour. She screams and faints.

> *Perhaps this reflects Janakikutty's own turbulence at the wedding. She perhaps empathises with Sarojini's emotional trauma as the groom ties the knot, marking a definite end to the relationship between Sarojini and Bhaskaran. Kunjathol's fierce transformation might reflect Janakikutty's resistance to these unpleasant feelings. This perhaps causes her to react with denial, triggering an episode of dissociation and aggression.*

Janakikutty's family members bring her home. Subsequent to the wedding, *Muthassi's* last rites are in progress. *Janakikutty* is unable to confront the trauma of *Muthassi's* death and remains in denial, switching to dissociation. A dissociated *Janakikutty* fantasizes *Muthassi* as flying away from the burning pyre towards freedom. *Janakikutty's* mother catches her dancing and is puzzled by her inappropriate exhilaration. Her father steps in and decides to get her psychiatric help and admits her to the hospital.

Janakikutty responds to the medications. There are brief hallucinations in response to the medication. *Kunjathol's* perception is no longer comforting to *Janakikutty*. Instead, it is terrifying and she reacts with fear to the perception. This fear perhaps reflects *Janakikutty's* discomfort at the aggressive transformation of her own personality and a need to come out of the aggressive and destructive behaviour that is against her basic nature. *Janakikutty* resents the idea of harming others and perhaps fears the acts of harm caused unknowingly by her own self.

Janakikutty now bids goodbye to *Kunjathol* with mixed feelings. She visualizes *Kunjathol*, the fantasy character who helped her tide over a traumatic phase by compensating for her vulnerability, walk away into thin air. Her attachment to this fantasy character causes her to cling on to the memory, refusing to believe it was all fantasy. Fortunately, *Bhaskaran* is around to comfort her and provide her warmth and companionship. *Janakikutty* shares her fantasy world with *Bhaskaran* and confesses as to how *Kunjathol* clung to her as a realistic perception for a long time.

The deep attachment to the fantasy character illustrates Janakikutty's inability to come out of attachments, real and virtual. It reflects the deep rooting of her fragile mind to relationships that fill the emotional void in her life.

The character of Janakikutty breathes life into the phenomenon of dissociation and fantasy that are awakened in a fragile mind as a coping response to trauma, shaping our attitude to the entity of dissociative disorders. The film sheds light on the psychological needs of such individuals and helps us empathize with them. The film teaches us to see the extraordinary ability of their minds to break free from the negativity of their circumstances in order to preserve their integrity for they cannot otherwise survive the assaults of an insensitive world. The film educates us on the infinite and overwhelming potential of the human mind that cannot be reduced to the confines of a psychiatric label.

BIBLIOGRAPHY

1. Omid Safi. November 6, 2014. 'The disease of being busy,' *On Being.* http://www.onbeing.org/blog/the-disease-of-being-busy/7023

2. Ruth Yvonne Pavlovic, Alexandar Mido Pavlovic. 'Dostoevsky and psychoanalysis – psychiatry in 19th-century literature.' *The British Journal of Psychiatry* Mar 2012, 200 (3) 181; **DOI:** 10.1192/bjp.bp.111.093823.

3. '10 pc Keralites suffer from mental disorders,' *English Mathrubhumi,* October 20, 2015.

    *http://english.mathrubhumi.com/news/kerala/10-pc-keralites-suffer-from-mental-*disorders-english-news-1.616506

4. Abraham H. Maslow, "Self-Actualizing People: A Study of Psychological Health." *Motivation and Personality.*(1987). 3rd ed., Chapter 11. New York: Harper and Row.

5. Carl Rogers, *On Becoming a Person* (1961) p. 350–1. Boston: Houghton Mifflin.

6. Freud, S. (1920). *Beyond the pleasure principle.* SE, 18: 1–64.

7. Freud, S. (1923). *The ego and the id.* SE, 19: 1–66.

8. Freud, A. (1937). *The Ego and the mechanisms of defense,* London: Hogarth Press and Institute of Psycho-Analysis.

9. McLeod, S. A. (2009). *Defense Mechanisms.* Retrieved from www.simplypsychology.org/defense-mechanisms.html

10. Vaillant, George E. (1977). *Adaptation to life.* Boston: Little, Brown. ISBN 0–316–89520–2.

11. Cramer, Phebe. (May 2006). *Protecting the Self.* The Guilford Press. p. 325. ISBN 9781593855284.

12. Lynne Namka (1996). *How to let go of your mad baggage.* Talk, Trust and Feel Therapeutics, Incorporated. ISBN-13: 978–0964216716

13. Clay Tucker-Ladd (2009). *Psychological Self-Help,* Chapter-7. Psych Central.com

    http://psychologicalselfhelp.org/Chapter7.pdf

14. Bevan, J.L. (2004). General partner and relational uncertainty as consequences of another person's jealousy expression. *Western Journal of Communication*, 68, 195–218.

15. James, W. (1892). *Psychology: The briefer course*. New York: Henry Holt.

16. Power, F. Clark; Khmelkov, Vladimir T. (1998). "Character development and self-esteem: Psychological foundations and educational implications." *International Journal of Educational Research*. **27** (7): 539–551.doi:10.1016/S0883–0355(97)00053–0

17. Barry, P. (2002). *Mental Health and Mental Illness*. (7th ed.) New York: Lippincott.

18. Rogers, Carl. (1959). "A theory of therapy, personality relationships as developed in the client-centered framework.." In (Ed.) S. Koch. *Psychology: A study of a science. Vol. 3: Formulations of the person and the social context*. New York: McGraw Hill.

19. Bandura, A. (1986). *Social foundations of thought and action: a social cognitive theory*. Englewood Cliffs, N.J.: Prentice-Hall.

20. Bandura, A. (2002). *Social cognitive theory of mass communication*. In J. Bryant & M. B. Oliver (Eds.), Media Effects: Advances in Theory and Research (pp. 94–124). New York, NY: Routledge.

21. Mischel, Walter; Shoda, Yuichi. (1995). "A cognitive-affective system theory of personality: Reconceptualizing situations, dispositions, dynamics, and invariance in personality structure." *Psychological Review*. **102** (2): 246–268.

22. Bee, Helen; Boyd, Denise. (March 2009). *The Developing Child* (12th ed.). Boston, MA: Pearson. ISBN 978–0-205–68593–6.

23. Crain, William (2011). *Theories of Development: Concepts and Applications* (6th ed.). Upper Saddle River, NJ: Pearson Education, Inc. ISBN 978–0-205–81046–8.

24. Tyson, Phyllis. 'A developmental line of gender identity, gender role, and choice of love object.' *Journal of the American Psychoanalytic Association*. Vol 30(1), 1982, 61–86.

25. Erikson [Sa]. Erik Erikson's 8 Stages of Psychosocial Development. [O]. http://web.cortland.edu/andersmd/ERIK/sum.html 98 Accessed on 2007/07/27

26. Erikson, E. H. (1968). Identity, Youth and Crisis. London: Norton & Company Inc.

27. Annandale E., Hunt K. (1990). Masculinity, femininity and sex: an exploration of their relative contribution to explaining gender differences in health. *Sociol. Health Illn.* 12, 24–46. 10.1111/1467–9566.ep10844865

28. Mayor E. Gender roles and traits in stress and health. *Frontiers in Psychology.* 2015;6:779. doi:10.3389/fpsyg.2015.00779.

29. Seligman, Martin E.P. (1984). "Chapter 11." *Abnormal Psychology.* W. W. Norton & Company. ISBN 0–393–94459-X

30. Bienenfeld, David (2006). "Personality Disorders." *Medscape Reference.* WebMD. Retrieved 10 January 2007.

31. Bockian, Neil R (2006). Depression in Histrionic Personality Disorder. Personality-guided therapy for depression. (pp. 169–186).

32. Pfohl, B. (1995). Histrionic personality disorder. The DSM IV Personality Disorders, 173–192.

33. *Histrionic Personality Disorder*, Encyclopedia of Mental Disorders

http://www.minddisorders.com/Flu-Inv/Histrionic-personality-disorder.html

34. Smith, E. R.; Mackie, D. M. (2007). *Social Psychology* (Third ed.). Hove: Psychology Press. ISBN 978–1-84169–408–5.

35. José-Vicente Bonet. *Sé amigo de ti mismo: manual de autoestima.* 1997. Ed. Sal Terrae. Maliaño (Cantabria, España). ISBN 978–84–293–1133–4

36. Adapted , Gill J. "Indispensable Self-Esteem." *Human Development.* **1**: 1980.

37. A. Leiva J. Y. Rodríguez L. Nohemy Carrasco M. Durán M. Portillo S. M. Lam. (2015). "Como influye el genero en la Autoestima de los Adolescentes" Online at *Universidad Nacional Autónoma de Honduras.*

38. Bonet Gallardo, L. Huertas Bailén, Amparo.(2015). "Feedback between self-esteem and digital activity in the adolescent group." *Universidad Autónoma de Barcelona.*

39. Michele S. Berk, Bernadette Grosjean, Heather D. Warnick. (May 2009). Beyond threats: Risk factors for suicide in borderline personality disorder. *Current Psychiatry*. Vol. 8, No. 5.

40. Gunderson, John G. (26 May 2011). "Borderline Personality Disorder." *The New England Journal of Medicine*. **364** (21): 2037–2042.

41. *Linehan, Marsha (1993). Cognitive-behavioral treatment of borderline personality disorder. New York: Guilford Press. ISBN 0–89862–183–6.*

42. *Manning, Shari (2011). Loving Someone with Borderline Personality Disorder. The Guilford Press. ISBN 978–1–59385–607–6.*

43. Koenigsberg HW, Harvey PD, Mitropoulou V, et al. (May 2002). "Characterizing affective instability in borderline personality disorder." *Am J Psychiatry*. **159** (5): 784–8.

44. Zanarini MC, Frankenburg FR, Reich DB, et al. (2000). "Biparental failure in the childhood experiences of borderline patients." *J Personal Disord*. **14** (3): 264–73.

45.   Raboteg-Saric Z.; Sakic M. (2014). "Relations of parenting styles and friendship quality to self-esteem, life satisfaction, & happiness in adolescents." *Applied Research in the Quality of Life*. **9**: 749–765.

46. Olsen, J. M.; Breckler, S. J.; Wiggins, E. C. (2008). *Social Psychology Alive* (First Canadian ed.). Toronto: Thomson Nelson. ISBN 978–0–17–622452–3.

47. Axmacher, Nikolai, et al. "Natural memory beyond the storage model: repression, trauma, and the construction of a personal past." *Frontiers in human neuroscience* 4 (2010): 211.

48. Sadock, B. J., & Sadock, V. A. (2004). *Kaplan and Sadock's concise textbook of clinical psychiatry*(2nd ed.). Philadelphia, PA: Lippincott Williams & Wilkins.

49. Fink, D. L. (1988). "Review of the book The shattered self: A psychoanalytic study of trauma." *Dissociation, 1*(4), 59–60.

50. Chu, J. A. (1991). The repetition-compulsion revisited: Reliving dissociated trauma.*Psychotherapy, 28*(2), 327–332.

51. Verhaeghe, P., & Vanheule, S. (2005). Actual neurosis and PTSD: The impact of the other.*Psychoanalytic Psychology, 22*(4), 493–507.

52. *Diagnostic and Statistical Manual (Fourth Edition), Text Revision* (DSM-IV-TR).

53. American Psychiatric Association. Diagnostic and Statistical Manual of Mental Disorders, Fourth Edition, Text Revision. Washington, DC: American Psychiatric Press, Inc.; 2000.

54. Loewenstein, R.J. (1991). Psychogenic amnesia and psychogenic fugue: A comprehensive review. In A. Tasman and S.M. Goldfinger (Eds.). *American Psychiatric Press Review of Psychiatry* Vol 10, pp.189–222. Washington, DC: American Psychiatric Press.

55. American Psychiatric Association (2000). *DSM-IV-TR* (4th ed.). American Psychiatric Press. p. 543. ISBN 0–89042–025–4.

56. Schacter, D. L., Gilbert, D. T., & Wegner, D.M. (2011). *Psychology: Second Edition*, pages 572–573. New York, NY: Worth.

57. Lynn, Steven J.; Rhue, Judith W. (1988). "Fantasy proneness: Hypnosis, developmental antecedents, and psychopathology." *American Psychologist.* **43**: 35–44.

58. Wilson, S. C. & Barber, T. X. (1983). "The fantasy-prone personality: Implications for understanding imagery, hypnosis, and parapsychological phenomena." In, A. A. Sheikh (editor), Imagery: *Current Theory, Research and Application* (pp. 340–390). New York: Wiley. ISBN 0471 092258. Republished (edited): Psi Research 1(3), 94 - 116.

59. Merckelbach, H. et al. (2001). The Creative Experiences Questionnaire (CEQ): a brief self-report measure of fantasy proneness. *Personality and Individual Differences*, vol. 31, 987–995.

60. Dalenberg, Constance J.; Brand, Bethany L.; Gleaves, David H.; et al. (2012). "Evaluation of the evidence for the trauma and fantasy models of dissociation" (PDF). *Psychological Bulletin.* **138** (3): 550–588

61. Simeon, D (2008). "Dissociative Identity Disorder." Merck & Co.

62. Lynn, SJ; Berg J; Lilienfeld SO; Merckelbach H; Giesbrecht T; Accardi M; Cleere C (2012). "14 - Dissociative disorders." In Hersen M; Beidel DC. *Adult Psychopathology and Diagnosis.* John Wiley & Sons. pp. 497–538. ISBN 1–118–13882–1.

63. Sadock, BJ; Sadock VA (2007). "Dissociative disorders — Dissociative identity disorder." *Kaplan & Sadock's synopsis of psychiatry: behavioral sciences/clinical psychiatry* (10th ed.). Philadelphia: Lippincott Williams & Wilkins. pp. 671–6. ISBN 978-0-7817-7327-0.

64. Maldonado, JR; Spiegel D (2008). "Dissociative disorders — Dissociative identity disorder (Multiple personality disorder)." In Hales RE; Yudofsky SC; Gabbard GO; with foreword by Alan F. Schatzberg. *The American Psychiatric Publishing textbook of psychiatry* (5th ed.). Washington, DC: American Psychiatric Pub. pp. 681–710. ISBN 978-1-58562-257-3.

65. Joseph, J.S. & Gray, M.J. (2008). Exposure Therapy for Posttraumatic Stress Disorder. *Journal of Behavior Analysis of Offender and Victim: Treatment and Prevention*, 1(4), 69–80 BAO.

Appendix: Film Bibliography

Serial No.	Year	Film	Script/ Screenplay	Direction	Book from which adapted
66	1988	Aranyakam	M.T. Vasudevan Nair	Hariharan	
67	1987	Thoovanathumbikal	P. Padmarajan	P. Padmarajan	Udakappola (Padmarajan)
68	2000	Mazha	Lenin Rajendran	Lenin Rajendran	Nashtapetta Neelambari (Madhavi kutty)
69	2002	Nandanam	Ranjith	Ranjith	
70	1996	Udyanapalakan	A.K.Lohithadas	Hari Kumar	
71	1996	Thooval Kottaram	A.K.Lohithadas	Sathyan Anthikad	
72	1987	Sreedharante Onnam Thirumurivu	Sreenivasan	Sathyan Anthikad	
73	1986	Namukku Parkkan Munthiri Thoppukal	P.Padmarajan	P.Padmarajan	Nammukku Gramangalil Chennu Rapparkkam (K.K. Sudhakaran)
74	1992	Yamanam	George Onakkoor	Bharath Gopi	Kamana (George Onakkoor)
75	1998	Sneham	T.A.Razak	Jayaraj	
76	1988	Kakkothikkavile Appooppan Thaadikal	Fazil	Kamal	
77	1984	Nokkethadoorathu Kannum Nattu	Fazil	Fazil	
78	1993	Valsalyam	A.K.Lohithadas	Cochin Haneefa	

(Contd.)

Serial No.	Year	Film	Script/ Screenplay	Direction	Book from which adapted
79	1993	Golanthara Vartha	Sreenivasan	Sathyan Anthikad	
80	2003	Manassinakkare	Ranjan Pramod	Sathyan Anthikad	
81	1994	Parinayam	M.T.Vasudevan Nair	Hariharan	
82	1994	Chakoram	A.K.Lohithadas	M.A.Venu	
83	1998	Kanmadam	A. K. Lohithadas	A. K. Lohithadas	
84	1992	Sargam	Hariharan & Chowallur Krishnankutty (dialogues)	Hariharan	
85	1986	Desatanakkilli Karayarilla	P.Padmarajan	P. Padmarajan	
86	1991	Bharatham	A. K. Lohithadas	Sibi Malayil	
87	1998	Oru Maravathoor Kanavu	Sreenivasan	Lal Jose	
88	1989	Kireedam	A. K. Lohithadas	Sibi Malayil	
89	1987	Thaniyavarthanam	A. K. Lohithadas	Sibi Malayil	
90	1989	Vadakkunokkiyanthram	Sreenivasan	Sreenivasan	
91	1990	Pavam Pavam Rajakumaran	Sreenivasan	Kamal	
92	1998	Chinthavishtayaya Shyamala	Sreenivasan	Sreenivasan	
93	1995	Mazhayethum Munpe	Sreenivasan	Kamal	
94	1993	Oru Kadankatha Pole	John Paul Puthusery	Joshy Mathew	
95	1988	Ulsavapittennu	John Paul Puthusery	Bharath Gopi	
96	1993	Manichithrathazhu	Madhu Muttam	Fazil	
97	1986	Sanmanassullavarkku Samadhanam	Sreenivasan	Sathyan Anthikkad	
98	1991	Ulladakkam	P.Balachandran	Kamal	
99	1994	Sudinam	Babu Janardhanan	Nissar	

(Contd.)

Serial No.	Year	Film	Script/ Screenplay	Direction	Book from which adapted
100	1998	Ennu Swantham Janakikutty	M. T. Vasudevan Nair	Hariharan	
101	1992	Savidham	John Paul	George Kithu	
102	1987	Neeyethra Dhanya	John Paul	Jesey	
103	1982	Chillu	Lenin Rajendran	Lenin Rajendran	
104	1998	Pranayavarnangal	Jayaraman Kadambaat and Sachithanandan Puzhankara	Sibi Malayil	
105	1994	Pavithram	P. Balachandran	T. K. Rajeev Kumar	
106	1989	Innale	Padmarajan	Padmarajan	
107	2005	Thanmathra	Blessy	Blessy	Padmarajan's short story "Orma"
108	2006	Vadakkumnathan	Gireesh Puthenchery	Shajoon Kariyal	
109	1986	Thalavattam	Nedumudi Venu & Priyadarshan (dialogues)	Priyadarshan	
110	1991	Mookilla Rajyathu	B. Jayachandran	Ashokan-Thaha	
111	1991	Kilukkam	Venu Nagavally	Priyadarshan